Better classroom relationships

Better classroom relationships

Maria Kecskemeti
University of Waikato

John Winslade
California State University San Bernardino

NZCER PRESS
New Zealand Council for Educational Research
PO Box 3237
Wellington
New Zealand

© Maria Kecskemeti and John Winslade, 2016

ISBN 978-1-927231-96-8

No part of the publication may be copied, stored or communicated in any form by any means (paper or digital), including recording or storing in an electronic retrieval system, without the written permission of the publisher.
Education institutions that hold a current licence with Copyright Licensing New Zealand may copy from this book in strict accordance with the terms of the CLNZ Licence.

A catalogue record for this book is available from the National Library of New Zealand

Designed by Smartwork Creative Ltd

Cover photograph © Wendy Drewery

Contents

Preface ... vii

Acknowledgements ... ix

Chapter 1   What is a relationship-centred approach? ... 1

Chapter 2   Loosening the grip of normal:
"I have got a sexual harassment case to deal with" ... 16

Chapter 3   The stance of curiosity:
"Don't lie to me. You were stalking her" ... 42

Chapter 4   Externalising conversations:
"A hundred baits were not enough to catch one fish" ... 63

Chapter 5   Problematising discourses of teaching and learning:
"I switch off because it is boring. It is your job to teach us anyway" ... 88

Chapter 6   A deconstructive approach to class meetings:
"There is too much talking. We get very little work done" ... 109

Chapter 7   A diffractive approach to thinking about professional practice and identity: "I knew I was a good teacher. I was teaching kids who were difficult to manage" ... 135

Chapter 8   Introducing the relationship-centred approach to teachers ... 159

References ... 172

Index ... 183

Figures

Figure 1: The process of normalising judgement — 14

Figure 2: Citational practices — 40

Figure 3: Two different approaches to inquiry — 61

Figure 4: Internalising and externalising — 83

Figure 5: Problematising discourses of teaching and learning — 107

Figure 6: Diffraction — 157

Tables

Table 1: Problematising dominant ideas — 132

Preface

The usual approaches to classroom relationships are either teacher centred or student centred. This book proposes a third way: relationship-centred classrooms.

Teacher-centred approaches to classroom relationships centralise and privilege the teacher's ideas about how things should be. This applies to the conduct of relationships as well as to curriculum delivery methods. The teacher is the absolute authority on everything. The classroom is organised to make things easy for the teacher.

Student-centred approaches, on the other hand, have been popular in progressive education. They privilege what students want and focus on the actualisation of the students' selves. Teachers are enjoined to trust students' 'natural' inclination to meet their own learning needs. Some authors claim that these approaches marginalise the teacher, who can withdraw so much into the background that she or he becomes almost invisible and insignificant, losing the necessary authority required to be taken seriously (see, for example, Furedi, 2009).

Of course, this is to draw a black-and-white distinction, and in real-life situations nothing is so simple. But it serves to emphasise a different approach that addresses what happens in relationships between teachers and students and makes events in this domain much more central. That is the intention of this book.

In a relationship-centred approach, both the teacher and the student are important and the emphasis shifts towards the quality of their interaction. What happens in that relationship either supports or hinders teaching and learning. The central question then becomes, "What are the relational conditions that optimise opportunities for learning?"

We are not suggesting that there are magic answers to what makes for a perfect classroom relationship. The field of any relationship is constantly shifting and dynamic. What we focus on instead are some principles of analysis and how to apply these in practical situations. To do so we draw on social constructionist theory, which is the theoretical perspective that concentrates most systematically on what gets produced through relational contexts.

Whatever approach a teacher might use (for example, strict or permissive), it is important to engage in constant evaluation of the effects of the relationship practice in order to maintain a relationship conducive to learning. Teachers' work is becoming increasingly complex in today's heterogeneous classrooms. They are required to achieve multiple objectives of inclusion, citizenship education, the development of key competencies, cultural responsiveness and raised achievement levels. The extent to which teachers are able to manage this level of complexity is largely dependent on their capacity to create the conditions in which students feel safe and successful, and in which teaching and learning can take place.

In addition to subject knowledge, teachers also need the communication and relationship skills to build mutual respect and establish a learning environment conducive to learning. An increasing number of researchers and teachers claim that this can be achieved through generic principles of relationship conduct and a few well-chosen relationship practices. This book proposes a version of such a generic approach, which is also a specific pedagogy of relationships.

This book was born out of the assumption that organising the learning process in a diverse classroom requires a theory and practice of relationship that is responsive to unpredictability and to the constantly shifting nature of interactions. It also requires a clear understanding of power relations that is context specific. Because the authors have thought carefully about these issues, this book will not just rehash existing texts on classroom management or behaviour modification. It traverses new territory and explains it carefully in a brief, readable account of theoretical principles, and then illustrates them in practice.

To our knowledge there are no other current books for teachers on classroom management and relationship practice that draw on poststructuralist theory and adapt narrative counselling strategies for educational rather than therapeutic purposes. We are conscious, therefore, of venturing into new territory. The rationale for doing so is that many current approaches to these issues lack comprehensive effectiveness or do not take sufficient account of important ethical concerns. In the end, though, our readers will judge the value of these pages in the use they put them to. We eagerly anticipate what you will do.

Acknowledgements

The authors would like to thank all those students, classroom teachers and colleagues who so willingly opened themselves over the past 15 years to the not-yet-known and allowed Maria to try the conversational moves and analytical frameworks with them while she was working to adapt these for classroom and other relational uses in schools. Each case example included in the book is based on actual situations, with names and some details changed in order to maintain anonymity.

Maria would like to thank the following colleagues: Associate Professor Wendy Drewery, who inspired her to apply poststructuralist and narrative ideas to relationship practices in schools, first as her university lecturer, and then as her doctoral supervisor; Barbara Slevin, Linda Tucker, Brenda Martin and Latu To'omaga, her former resource teacher colleagues, who provided unwavering support for and belief in both the ideas and Maria's use of them in the early stages of experimentation; Bernice Cavanagh, Kathleen Kaveney, and Sheridan Gray, with whom she worked on a 3-year restorative project and who made significant contributions to the development of deconstructive class meetings, but also many of the other practices introduced in the book; Dr Carol Hamilton, with whom she developed circle conversations as a tool of intra-active pedagogy in initial teacher education; and her co-author, Professor John Winslade, who made the writing of this book seem easy by contributing his vast experience and knowledge of postmodern ideas and narrative counselling. Maria is indebted to all her colleagues, both at the University of Waikato and in the primary and secondary schools she has worked in, for the professional conversations they have had with her.

Maria also thanks her extended family: her daughters, Judit Berta and Mariska Kecskemeti, their partners, Pai Tuilaepa and Jason Zhu, and her grandchildren, Daunte and Peyton Tuilaepa, for their support and patience during this project, and her sister, Zsuzsa Molnar, who so kindly offered to free her from all housework in the final stages of writing that Maria completed in Hungary while on study leave.

John would like to thank those who have formed a community of interest around his efforts in growing the larger project, of which this text forms a part. In particular, that means his partner in life and family and in professional work, Lorraine Hedtke, and his abiding friend, Gerald Monk.

He also acknowledges his debt to his colleagues at California State University San Bernardino and at the University of Waikato: Todd Jennings, Daniel Stewart, Michelle Myers, Pascale Claus, and, recently, Shawn Patrick and John Beckenbach, all in San Bernardino as well as Wendy Drewery, Kathie Crocket, Wally MacKenzie, Elmarie Kotzé and Paul Flanagan in New Zealand. He also acknowledges the value of many conversations with those who work at San Bernardino City Unified School District, especially Henry Yzaguirre.

John has two children who are trained teachers, Zane Winslade and Joanna Winslade. For him, a sense of their potential interest and their stories of practice have hovered over the writing of this book. John's other son, Benjamin Winslade, and his wife, Tania Winslade, have two young children, Alexa and Kaea, for whom this book represents John's hope for their educational future. May they get to benefit from relationship-centred learning environments! His daughter Addison Davidove is a student of similar ideas in other contexts and is always up for a stimulating conversation about how to apply them.

John has also benefited from holding in mind the learning needs of his students at California State University San Bernardino, who are studying to be counsellors, teachers or administrators.

Finally, he would like readers to indulge him a moment longer while he acknowledges his co-author, Maria Kecskemeti. She is, in large measure, responsible for driving this project. It grew out of her PhD dissertation, supervised by Wendy Drewery. It also grew out of Maria's professional practice. She has, therefore, lived intimately with these practices for some time. While John has been interested in taking poststructuralist and narrative ideas into schools, Maria took these ideas more directly into the practice of teaching. She has proved easy to work with because she has kept her promises with regard to deadlines and has taken the initiative in drafting many parts of this text. John's role has been to add to the initiatives Maria has taken. He is grateful for her drive and creativity.

We are delighted to include a photo taken by Wendy Drewery on the cover of the book. We thank Ray Prebble for his insightful editorial comments that helped us further improve the clarity of our arguments. Many of the ideas and practices introduced in the book have been shaped to a great extent by the unique perspective that Professor Bronwyn Davies has put forward about relationships in schools in her articles, book chapters and books, which we have used extensively as references.

Maria Kecskemeti
Hamilton, New Zealand, December 2015

John Winslade
Redlands, California, USA, December 2015

Chapter 1 What is a relationship-centred approach?

Matt's story

Matt had only been at his new school for a month, but he had already come to the attention of both teachers and peers. His peers thought he was 'crazy' because he usually responded to attempts to involve him in conversations or games with grumpiness, shrugging his shoulders or some rude words. A simple enquiry about how he was going would often get, "It's none of your business!" Matt seemed to be angry all the time. If anyone tried to be humorous with him, about school or a teacher, he was likely to misunderstand it as teasing. He ended up chasing his classmates and issuing warnings about how he would bash them after school. Matt had not made any friends and most of his classmates had given up on him.

His teachers found him difficult to manage in class. When he was asked to contribute to a discussion, or to answer a question, he said, "No". If his teachers insisted, he often stormed out of class or kicked a chair. When he found the task difficult he ripped up his exercise book or paper and threw it in the rubbish bin, muttering swear words under his breath.

Teachers' usual responses

Matt is an example of a student who frequently responds to instructions and requests with defiance and non-compliance. Few teachers or students find him likeable. He is also a student whose teachers have tried multiple interventions with the purpose of changing his behaviours. In what follows we describe each of the interventions Matt's various teachers and schools have tried, along with some of the relational and other outcomes they produced. The order of presentation does not necessarily reflect the order of implementation. Rather, we have listed the interventions used on Matt on a continuum, moving from punitive towards restorative approaches.

Zero tolerance and punitive approaches

Some of Matt's current teachers would prefer the school use a zero tolerance approach with Matt or institute harsher punishments. In order to nip Matt's dramatic interruptions in the bud, these teachers frequently chose to send him out of class or refer him to a senior administrator. They often did this at the beginning of a lesson or when they suspected he might be in a bad mood. In addition, the zero tolerance advocates wanted him out of their school, and they stood Matt down for 3 days twice in the previous month. The general opinion among these teachers was that Matt should not be given more chances but should be suspended or expelled, because he wrecked lessons and interrupted the learning of others. Though Matt's current school principal was against zero tolerance, for the criticism it has received for opening up pathways to prison and frequently criminalising mild transgressions (Skiba & Peterson, 1999; Skiba, Michael, Caroll Nardo, & Peterson, 2002), she was finding it hard to convince a group of teachers on her staff.

Behaviour modification

Matt had also been on an individual behaviour modification programme that included strategies based on applied behaviour analysis, along with teaching him social skills and emotional literacy. The aim had been to replace Matt's problematic behaviours over time with acceptable ones through his behaviour specialist teacher and subject teachers using positive and negative reinforcement. Matt received rewards for behaving in desirable ways (for example, stickers that could be exchanged for free time or a preferred activity). Punishments were also applied, such as withdrawing privileges (for example, free computer time) in order to deter him from disrupting lessons. In his previous school a similar individualised programme had been accompanied by a medical intervention. Matt had been diagnosed with ADHD[1] and was put on Ritalin. His mother had stopped the medication, citing bad side-effects, such as internal shaking and sleeplessness. Matt was currently receiving social skills training from a specialist teacher, both individually and, on occasions, in small groups.

Positive behaviour
On the less intensive end of the continuum of behaviour management interventions we might find what is called a positive behaviour approach (Rogers, 2002, 2011). This was what one of Matt's more tolerant teachers, Ms Smith, used consistently, not only with Matt but with all her students. Ms Smith claimed that she had not felt the need to send Matt out of the classroom and/or refer him to senior administration.

The strategies within this approach are designed to help establish, with the least possible interruption to the lesson and in the short term, the kind of classroom order that is deemed necessary by the teacher or school for teaching and learning to occur. The simple, easy-to-use strategies recommended by Rogers include behaviour description, behaviour direction, rule reminder, directed choice, partial agreement and deferred consequence, which, in Ms Smith's interpretation looked like the following.

If Matt was off task, fiddling with an object instead of writing in his book, Ms Smith would use a *behaviour description* and a *behaviour direction*, saying, "Matt, you are playing with your phone. Eyes and ears this way, thanks." If Matt said, "No," to a request to contribute to a discussion with a grumpy tone, Ms Smith would say, "Matt, I can understand that you are upset about someone being mean to you (*partial agreement*), but remember our rules about participation. In this class, everyone is expected to contribute" (*rule reminder*, with rules referred to as 'our').

If Matt continued to refuse, Ms Smith would repeat the rule reminder, but adding a *directed choice*: "You could say what you think now or we could come back to you at the end." If Matt still insisted on staying out of the activity, she would use a *deferred consequence*: "If you decide not to participate, then I will have to follow it up in your own time."

Used with calm consistency with everyone, Ms Smith claimed these strategies were enough to keep Matt in her class and avoid referral to senior management.

Restorative and counselling-type interventions
Matt's social worker, John, preferred to use a restorative approach and to take up a listening rather than advice-giving stance. John often visited Matt's home and had informal conversations with both Matt's mother, Malia, and Matt. Recently he had found out that Malia had been struggling to find work as her English was not very good. She also had told him that Matt would often eat up all the bread from the kitchen cupboard, leaving nothing for her.

John believed that when Matt was defiant at home, Malia relied on his uncle to 'discipline' him, which was a term for giving Matt a serious hiding, for which John had referred the family to child protection agencies. The family had very few possessions and were struggling to make ends meet. Matt told John a number of times how misunderstood he felt, both at home and at school. He was scared of his uncle and angry at his mother for leaving their home country, where they used to have a better life.

He carried his worries about his home life to school, and that was why he was finding it hard to relax and to be kind to the other students. He also found it hard to cope with the work and did not want to embarrass himself in front of the other kids. Matt had also been referred to the school counsellor in order to learn anger management skills.

In addition, Matt's head teacher had recently called a whole-class restorative meeting with the intention of wanting to improve the relationships Matt had with his classmates. At the start, this meeting resembled the conversations Matt has had with John, his social worker and with his counsellor. Both Matt and his classmates were listened to and they were able to tell why they had felt hurt by the other. However, the meeting very much focused on what everyone's feelings were, rather than on underlying beliefs that might have shaped both Matt's and his classmates' negative responses to each other. The meeting ended with class members being invited to give individual advice to Matt. It is not surprising that Matt felt as if he had been in court and had been humiliated.

What can we make of Matt's story and his teachers' responses?

In the zero tolerance approach the problem was located solely in Matt. He was judged to fall outside the category of 'good student' and was deemed to present a risk to the school and to the other students. The main strategy in this approach was, therefore, the segregation of Matt from his peers and his exclusion from both the social and academic life of the classroom, even if temporarily.

It is much like how criminals are segregated from the normal members of society. He was expected to change his behaviours while away from others and without much support. Matt's actions were not considered in the context of the complex relational dynamics of the classroom. Within this approach it would be incomprehensible to entertain the idea that his angry outbursts might at times be reasonable—or at least understandable—responses to bullying or provocations and an expression of his hurt. No attempt was made to examine the system of power relationships in the classroom. It was only Matt who was found lacking in social skills. Even a remedial approach, offering training to Matt in social skills, was considered pointless. Teachers were closed to the possibility of trying to reintegrate him into the classroom. While the punishment dished out to Matt might demonstrate the power of the law (in this case the school's rules) and the power of authority or the state (Noguera, 2003), showing the deterrent qualities of disciplinary power, it would do nothing to rework existing power relationships.

Matt was finding it extremely difficult to re-establish himself as a member of his class after the days he had spent being suspended. He had missed some of the happenings that his peers kept referring to in their conversations and felt unable to contribute. He felt even more hurt and was often more grumpy than before, reinforcing the image that his peers and several of his teachers had of him.

The individual behaviour modification programme had yielded several positive outcomes, with Matt learning accepted behaviours and stopping those that often put him in trouble. However, making him the object of such an intervention also placed him in the category of 'behaviourally disabled'. Although establishing his categorical difference from the other students through assessment and treatment might have been necessary to secure the provision of interventions from a behaviour specialist, such categorisation separated him from the rest of the students, locating him at the negative end of the good student / bad student binary. Once his difference had been made into a problem, the possibilities were opened up for him to be further pathologised and to be rendered not only academically or behaviourally but also morally inferior. His chances of being singled out and bullied were increased. Matt's frequent absence from class as a result of being pulled out for remedial sessions with the behaviour specialist confirmed his difference from his peers and made him an easy target for being bullied for being 'dumb'.

No similar negative effects had so far been identified for the positive behaviour interventions that Ms Smith used. This could be because she did not just use them with Matt but with all the students whenever she thought classroom order needed to be re-established. She had reported to the principal that Matt's on-task time had increased.

The conversations the social worker had been having with Matt and the sessions with the school counsellor had provided a validating experience for Matt, as he felt he was taken seriously and was listened to. However, while these interventions might have eased Matt's stress and improved his overall confidence and wellbeing, they did not go far enough to change the power dynamics of Matt's class. The social worker and counsellor mostly worked with Matt individually and could do little to create a legitimate position for him among the good students in the classroom. While Matt enjoyed these conversations, he had to leave the class to have them, as he did for his remedial sessions, which again reinforced his difference from others.

Both the social worker and the counsellor might have become witnesses to parts of Matt's life that were usually hidden from teachers. The codes of confidentiality, however, usually prevented both counsellors and social workers from sharing such information with teachers. Yet this information shed light on how his circumstances and social conditions might have made the demands of school, and what it took to be a good student, almost impossible to bear.

Even the restorative class meeting that had been called to improve relationships between Matt and his classmates turned into moralising and condemning him, because he did not fit the school's and other students' notion of what constituted an emotionally literate and socially skilled person (Ecclestone, 2007; Ecclestone & Hayes, 2009; Leach & Lewis, 2013). Matt had told his counsellor that he would not want to participate in such a meeting again.

A more relational approach

While several of the above-described interventions could at times be useful with some students, with Matt they produced detrimental effects, achieving the opposite of what the participants intended, with the exception of the positive behaviour approach. We have highlighted above, albeit somewhat artificially, those features of these processes that we think increased the possibility of resistance and hurt and decreased the possibility of collaboration.

All of these interventions (or their various implementations) were based on a liberal-humanist notion of the autonomous individual, which means they all located the problem in the individual rather than in the relational dynamics of the group. Even a restorative meeting, which had the potential to be different, could end up focusing on the effects of hurt on individuals, as opposed to examining the complex relational context of the classroom and the socially available ideas that reproduced conflict and harmful behaviours.

Normalising, or normalisation, is at the heart of this individualistic rather than relational approach (Davies, 2013; Davies, De Schauwer, Claes, De Munck, Van de Putte, & Vertichele, 2013). It was because of this process that Matt had been segregated from others, perceived as different, and felt hurt and humiliated.

What does this mean? It means that schools, and societies, create norms or rules that prescribe both acceptable conduct and the qualities of the kinds of persons who are judged to be normal or proper citizens. Norms establish categories, which divide people into normal and abnormal, or good and bad. Norms also create a desire to belong to and to be recognised as belonging to accepted categories. Judith Butler (2004a) argues that we all depend on norms or categories for our existence and need to be recognised as belonging to them.

Compliance with the accepted norms of a community earns recognition as a person. Non-compliance—being different from the norm and not fitting its categories—can deprive a person of a viable existence. The desire to fit normative categories creates two kinds of vulnerabilities. On the one hand, we are dependent on others for recognition, as it is others who will decide whether our behaviours constitute compliance and whether we deserve to be acknowledged or not. On the other hand, we can also be vulnerable to our own judgement as we internalise norms and want to live according to their specifications, constantly measuring whether we have lived up to them or not.

What are some of the consequences of such an individualistic approach, and how can the normalisation process play out in relationships? Any difference from the norm becomes a problem, because a norm "comes to be what is expected, and the expected slides quickly into morality. It becomes ought. The normative becomes the socially approved way of being" (Davies, 2013, p. 21). Normative categories are exclusive because they rely, for their definition, on what they are not: people, qualities and behaviours that do not fit them.

While norms can provide a necessary certainty for how we should act in particular situations, they can also obstruct or prevent change. Judgements by others about whether a person is compliant or not with a norm can become fixed descriptions about a person's qualities and attributes. Once considered different and excluded from the category of 'normal', it can be very hard for anyone to gain recognition.

The location of the problem in Matt and his temporary separation and segregation from others based on his differences (for instance, during his stand-down or suspension, his individual behaviour and counselling sessions) marked him out as pathologically different from the rest of the class, whose behaviours were considered worthy of recognition. Being stood down for a few days not only temporarily deprived Matt of schooling, but made it virtually unmanageable and impossible for him to weave himself back into the complex web of relationships and connections that had been established in his absence.

We think the fact that most of these previously described interventions did not achieve the desired positive relational outcomes that Matt's teachers, social worker and counsellor had hoped for is not the fault of any individual. Rather, these negative effects are due to the dominance and strong pull of ideas and practices that privilege and support the process of normalising, that centralise the autonomous individual, rather than introducing a relational view of problems. Matt was made to be solely responsible for all his relational problems. Ms Smith, on the other hand, did not locate the problem solely in Matt, because she treated everyone the same, although she did not go as far as addressing the power dynamics of the classroom.

Even the restorative meeting, which had deliberately set out to be relational and to treat problems as a collective responsibility, had deteriorated into moralising and targeting him rather than trying to find collective solutions. A restorative meeting can be hijacked by these ideas, which is testament to how firmly they are embedded in our everyday practices. They have become so taken for granted that it is hard to replace them with something else and to conduct relationships differently.

The particular relational approach we introduce in this book, we believe, helps reduce the potential for unhelpful outcomes—for Matt and for students similar to him. It is an approach that moves away from the notion of persons as individuals separate from others. Instead, it considers them not just as interacting, but as *intra-acting* with everything else, persons, objects or other living things included. Interaction is an exchange between two autonomous individuals. Intra-action, on the other hand, means that different persons, their environments and the objects, thoughts and living things in those environments, interfere with and affect each other in often unpredictable ways (Barad, 2007; Davies & Gannon, 2012).

Within an intra-actional view, problematic behaviours (for example, Matt's angry response or his grumpiness) will not only belong to him but will be produced as a response to a look by someone else, a tone of voice that might resemble the way his uncle speaks to him when he beats him, or by seeing someone eating a sandwich when he knows there is no more bread at home in the cupboard.

We think that much more is needed than just good intentions to achieve a shift from the judgemental moralising that "responds to the failings of individual autonomous selves" (Davies, 2014b, p. 738). We believe that two key assumptions and the conscious use of a number of ways of speaking and relational practices can help implement this relational approach more easily. We will introduce each of them in more detail in the following chapters, but let us describe them briefly here.

The relational approach we use in this book

The following two key assumptions are the basis of all the relationship practices described in this book:

- the importance of being recognised and validated as a person
- the importance of challenging ideas circulating in the social context that exclude, oppress and disadvantage persons.

The importance of being recognised and validated as a person means that we advocate relationship practices that reduce the effects of, or try to minimise opportunities for, normalising. How is it possible to do this? The specific relationship principles and ways of speaking or conversational moves that can help achieve this purpose are introduced in Chapters 2, 3 and 4.

Chapter 2 discusses the importance of paying conscious attention to the productive power of language, and the process of producing undesirable subjects by the ways in which we speak repeatedly about a person. Ways of avoiding totalising as opposed to fixing someone as the problem are introduced. Instead of segregating and separating a person because of his or her difference and making difference a problem, within a relational approach difference is considered to be normal. This means that we consciously and deliberately explore people's different views and the meanings they might make of events. This requires us to take a *curious* stance and to give up our assumptions about what is normal in order to include not only dominant but also other knowledges.

Chapter 3 contrasts the stances of curiosity and certainty and shows, through examples, how it is possible to generate conversations that increase possibilities for recognition, because they stretch the boundaries of normal through listening to the *not-yet-known*. We also show how it is possible to increase a person's capacity to be open towards, and be affected by, others.

Chapter 4 introduces externalising, another conversational move that helps avoid totalising and permanently fixing difference from the norm as problematic.

The second major assumption on which this book is based is the importance of challenging ideas circulating in the social context that exclude, oppress and disadvantage persons. According to this assumption, the normalisation process mentioned previously is informed by socially available ideas or discourses, which prescribe what kind of relationship practices, identities, persons, qualities and categories are considered normal, acceptable and preferable. Some of these ideas can become so taken for granted that their oppressive and exclusive effects are no longer noticed.

Because people take up their identities and conduct their relationships according to such ideas, it seems feasible that they also shape relationships in an indirect, not-obvious way. In order to change unhelpful relationship patterns, it is not enough to change how we relate to other individuals. We need to problematise, challenge and unpack the ideas or discourses that call harmful ways of interacting into being. Without changing the hidden assumptions that guide relationship practice, lasting change cannot be achieved.

In addition, discourses are produced and reproduced not by a single individual but by all of us. Therefore, problems are also located in discourses and not individuals. Matt was not grumpy and angry because he is a bad person, but because he was using a socially available response to hurt, which is also a more legitimate expression of being a male and being strong than crying is. Taking a relational approach means going beyond seeing everyone in Matt's class as separate entities. Instead of blaming individuals like Matt, within a relational approach we would examine discourses on which Matt and his classmates and the teachers in his school draw, identifying the ways they shape relationships. This means that we create opportunities for both teachers and students to engage with each other differently in the collaborative examination and challenging of hidden assumptions.

Chapter 5 describes how it is possible to be sensitised to recognising hidden assumptions that support conflict, particularly ideas about the purpose of schooling and the learning process.

Chapter 6 introduces a class meeting process that helps teachers and students to collaboratively examine and critique ideas about learning that place them in conflict with their own best intentions. The process also supports students' learning of key competencies.

Chapter 7 demonstrates the use of teacher support groups and teachers critiquing ideas and notions of professionalism together in support of developing their professional identity and ethics.

Finally, **Chapter 8** describes one possible way of introducing these practices into a school.

One of us teaches beginning teachers, whose common response to any relationship or other problems is a request for specific strategies and interventions. They say that they need to learn skills and have specific knowledge that will help them cater for the needs of each of their students. However, when they talk about how they might obtain the knowledge required, they do it with anxiety about whether they will be able to have access to the right kind of professional learning opportunities, resources and support from management. Some beginning teachers admit they are scared because they do not know whether they will be able to keep up.

We think this fear and anxiety is the product of a particular notion of teaching and of the teacher's role on which these student teachers draw: technical solutions are the most important part of the job. We are not saying that technical knowledge is not important. However, within such a conceptualisation of teaching, one can only be either competent and effective or incompetent. Having (or not having) a particular kind of knowledge is the only measure of a teacher's value.

We believe that in order to be able to respond to the diversity of today's classrooms and constantly changing relational dynamics it is useful to have a different conceptualisation of the teacher's role, one that calls for teachers to develop their capacity to sit with uncertainty and to respond to ethical dilemmas by using an analytical framework, as opposed to using technical knowledge. Within this view, a teacher is comfortable with the uncertainty that every relationship encounter might present and she or he accepts that it might not be possible to know at the start what the solution to a relationship problem might be and how particular relationships will play out. The knowledge that will be required to change a relationship will emerge from the process of engagement with others—with students, colleagues and parents.

This book introduces some possible processes for engaging with students and other adults differently from the usual modes of interacting in the classroom or in a school. Although we provide examples of conversational moves and processes, this book is not intended to be used as a 'how to' resource. Rather, our aim is to show that other possibilities and alternatives to conflict can be opened up when teachers approach a difficult situation with some specific relationship principles in mind and by thinking about the situation using a particular theoretical framework and the notion of discourse. None of the processes introduced can be used in a script-like manner; there is more work required to adapt them to specific situations.

The ideas and practices described in this book do not require teachers to completely throw out assessment, diagnosis and all the categorial labels that are inevitable within an individualistic approach to problems. The specialist knowledge applied in response to students' differences—whether those differences are to do with learning or behaviour difficulties, special needs or disabilities—can help students to participate more fully in a classroom community. However, within the relational approach that we recommend, we ask teachers to move away from "judging the failings of individual autonomous selves" (Davies, 2014b, p. 738) that is often involved in assessment and diagnostic practices, and that, in addition to informing interventions, can easily be used as moral judgements about students.

We ask teachers to engage in a completely different ethics that compels them to ask how things are possible. It is, as Davies (2014b) proposes, "a provocation to think differently and to become different—to move away from moral judgment and toward ethics" (p. 738) in encounters with students, colleagues and parents. It is also a move away from the binary of good/bad, becoming instead open to other possibilities that might emerge in a particular relationship if we consciously set out to avoid normalising and if we are willing to problematise (make harder) those ideas in the social context that place us in opposition to each other.

Summary of main points in Chapter 1

- Common responses to challenging behaviour include zero tolerance and punishment, behaviour modification, positive behaviour support, restorative class meetings, and counselling.
- All of these approaches usually assume that problems lie inside the

individual student, rather than in relational dynamics.
- A relational approach pays attention to the process of normalisation, through which school communities establish norms and then categories of persons as good or bad students.
- These categories divide people into normal and abnormal, or good and bad.
- Norms allow certainty, but also lead to judgements of some persons as abnormal.
- Everyone needs to be recognised as belonging to socially accepted categories.
- Students who are not included in accepted categories find it hard to establish a viable existence.
- Helping students change challenging behaviours starts from treating as important every student's need to be recognised and validated as a person.
- It is also important to challenge ideas circulating in the social context that exclude, oppress and disadvantage persons.

Figure 1: The process of normalising judgement

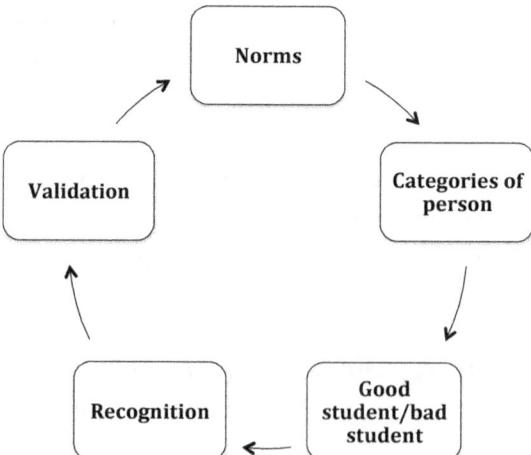

Exercise

Reflect on or discuss the following.

1. Can you think of situations you have encountered that resemble Matt's story?
2. In your experience, what are the limits of the usual individualistic approaches to responding to problematic student behaviour (zero tolerance, behaviour modification, positive behaviour support, certain uses of restorative class meetings, counselling)? How much do the limits you have experienced echo what this chapter is describing?
3. In relational terms, how do you explain why Matt felt hurt about being singled out?
4. Can you think of other examples in your own school in which students are commonly responded to in terms of categories?
5. At first glance, what appeals to you about thinking in more relational terms?

Endnote

1   Attention deficit hyperactivity disorder.

Chapter 2 Loosening the grip of normal: "I have got a sexual harassment case to deal with"

Introduction

In pursuit of a relationally responsive approach to classroom relationships we need to focus on linguistic performances. After all, it is not possible to conduct relationships without using language. However, language often comes to us ready-made. It is easy, therefore, to use it without reflection in ways that do damage. This chapter will illustrate how that can happen.

It focuses primarily on practices of naming: how persons and actions are named. How students, in particular, are repeatedly talked about (or named) is referred to here (following Davies, 2008, p. 173) as "ongoing repetitive citations", or citational practices. These practices cite students as certain types of person. Citational practices have strong impacts on how students can think about themselves and how they can act. The names given to events, actions, behaviours and people set up particular relationships and practice sequences. In the process, students are produced by the words of others as the kind of person they are cited to be. This person might have characteristics that are recognised as desirable or as undesirable. Those who are produced and made recognisable as undesirable persons are likely to be subject to mechanisms of exclusion.

Positioning people through the use of such citational practices as undesirable is not inevitable, however. It can be ruptured, and *lines of flight* (Deleuze, 1988; Winslade, 2009), that escape into other ways of speaking, can be found. For this reason, the concept and practice of *re-positioning* will also be introduced, to show how an utterance that seeks out difference, and invites students into speaking positions, can lead to the performance of different narratives. The chapter begins with the scenario of an actual situation which will be analysed below.

Sexual harassment or silly behaviour

During lunch interval in a primary school a group of seven or eight 6-year-olds decided to have a game of pulling down each other's pants. Judging from their loud giggling, which at times reached a crescendo of hysterical laughter, the children were enjoying themselves. This unusual boisterousness caught one duty teacher's attention, who decided to check out what was happening. The children were so immersed in their game that they did not even notice the duty teacher approaching their corner of the playground. Kate, the duty teacher who decided to intervene, firmly but calmly asked the children to stop what she qualified on the spot as a silly game. She also asked them to tidy their clothes, after which she promptly redirected them to another activity. The children complied and they spent the rest of their interval playing with balls and climbing on the monkey bars. Kate, who had only been a teacher for 2 years, was really pleased that the children followed her instructions without resistance. She even praised them for their wise choice of activities, post correction. She was confident she had addressed the problem behaviour competently and efficiently. She was also convinced that no further adult intervention was required, unless the children repeated the same silly behaviour.

It was usual teacher practice in this school to share with colleagues and senior managers any incidents that required a teacher to intervene and 'discipline' a child. Names of children who had temporarily transgressed school rules would be registered in morning briefings or in informal exchanges between staff, even when, according to the teachers involved, the children's transgressions had been dealt with in a satisfactory manner. Bringing incidents to the attention of colleagues was believed by most teachers to be an enactment of care. Children whose names were mentioned repeatedly received extra attention, and support was organised for them if their teachers thought the children might need it to stay out of trouble. Kate observed this custom and reported the pants-pulling she had had to stop, adding that the children were "just being silly", but that they had realised it and made good choices afterwards. She thought this was the end of the matter, just as on other similar occasions, when children corrected their behaviours after being reminded of the rules they had broken.

However, in this particular instance, Sue, one of the school's three deputy principals, had a different view on the matter. She asked for the names of all involved and announced to the staff that, in her opinion, what had happened should be termed sexual harassment. The other members of the senior management team had no objection to her interpretation, and Sue, who was in charge of discipline, proceeded to follow up the incident.

After a lengthy investigation, which included an interview with each participant in the game, Sue concluded that it was one particular child, Harry, who must have been the instigator of the 'pants-pulling game'. Though several teachers argued, first, that Harry was not playing this game on his own and therefore his 'partners in crime' had also contributed to the situation, and, second, that the children's actions could not be classified as sexual harassment, these arguments could not deter Sue from issuing her final verdict: there was a sexual harassment case to deal with. Sue singled out Harry, and only him, as needing an intervention, which included a referral to the Child, Youth and Family service.

During a subsequent investigation Harry's mother, Linda, was visited and questioned by social workers. At one point during the investigation the possibility of removing her son from her care was raised by one of the social workers. Linda's relationship with the school deteriorated, and she stopped participating in school activities as a parent helper.

Sue's insistence on calling the children's actions 'sexual harassment' produced further, most likely unintended but nevertheless detrimental, effects. While the investigation had been going on, several stories had emerged and had been repeatedly circulated in the staffroom about Harry's family. One of these stories implied the possibility of sexual abuse and imagined that it must have been committed against Harry by his brother or mother. His easy access to pornographic content, either videos or magazines allegedly owned by his brother, was cited as a reason for his behaviours, which, by this stage, were categorised as both pathological, and, given the assumed situation at home, inevitable.

Harry was placed under increased and constant teacher surveillance in the playground. He noticed that the duty teachers were watching him more intensely. So, instead of immersing himself in games as before, he kept looking in their direction, as if wanting to check that they approved of what he was doing. The investigation was concluded after 2 months. The school was informed that no evidence of abuse or neglectful parenting had been found. Therefore, Harry's case was closed. Linda was relieved but she told a teacher that she would be unable to trust the school again. In the end, she decided to enrol Harry at another school.

Kate, the duty teacher, and several other members of staff quietly continued to be unhappy with Sue's decision. They believed that their professional judgement had been called into question and they had also felt sidelined in the decision-making process about the school's response to Harry's and the other students' behaviour. These teachers would have liked a meeting where the whole staff were given an opportunity to have a conversation about which behaviours of 6-year-olds should warrant serious concern and which behaviours should be responded to in a low-key manner. It seemed to Kate that some of her colleagues who had agreed with Sue had become more 'cocky' and loud in subsequent staff meetings and informal discussions, as if they had no doubts whatsoever about the truth of their views. Kate believed these actions had been intended to remind her that she had been wrong.

What can we make of Harry's story and of the intervention chosen?

Kate interpreted Harry's actions differently from Sue. Their different interpretations and their subsequent references to the events—as silly behaviour or as sexual harassment—were informed by different assumptions about what children should or should not be allowed to do at the age of 6 years. According to the assumptions from which Kate drew, consenting children of the same age playing a game of exposing each other's bottoms could be considered normal and within the range of behaviours that should only warrant a low-key reprimand and redirection but should not be of serious concern. The assumptions that Sue drew upon to guide her actions deemed the same behaviours to be the symptoms of abuse that should immediately ring alarm bells and warrant a protective intervention. Since these two views were impossible to reconcile, they ended up in competition with one another.

It is probably not surprising that, in the end, the trajectory of what followed was defined by the meaning given to the events by one of the deputy principals, a person positioned higher in the school hierarchy than classroom teachers. Harry was referred to the Child, Youth and Family service, which routinely investigates child abuse. The other children who had also participated in the pants-pulling game received no intervention because a senior manager deemed it unnecessary. Once sexual harassment had become the privileged interpretation of the children's actions, an avalanche of far-reaching effects was triggered. We now try to make sense of how the term 'sexual harassment' affected the main participants, without claiming to account for all the possible effects of this powerful term. These effects, more often than not, were also long-lasting.

Linda was disturbed, first, that Sue, rather than having a conversation with her, had chosen to engage an agency outside the school. She felt hurt and angry and she believed no parent should fear losing a child as she had done, when the possibility of removing Harry from her care and placing him in foster care had been raised by social workers. She was accused of wrongdoing when she believed both herself and her son to be innocent. For those of us who have not been at the receiving end of such accusations, it might be hard to comprehend the intensity of her emotional responses to the school's actions.

Linda had been a parent helper at the school during school outings. She would often supervise a small group of children while they travelled on the train or by bus to the museum, the city library or the swimming pool. During the investigation she felt unable to turn up to accompany the children to their twice-weekly swimming lessons in the local swimming pool. The swimming lessons had been a highlight of her week, because she was training to become a swimming coach herself. As a parent helper she had opportunities to observe and learn from other coaches.

Linda told a trusted teacher that she simply could not pretend to look cheerful and enthusiastic, as if nothing had happened, which she felt she had to do for the children's sake. She was afraid that even just a glimpse of Sue could easily trigger her to cry in front of the children. She did not want to have to explain herself to them and she did not want Harry to see her distress.

Linda decided to excuse herself from her duties as parent helper for that term, in spite of being convinced that Sue and some other teachers might consider her unreliable. She missed the children very much and at times even contemplated dropping out of her training. In the mornings, when she dropped Harry off to school, she frequently caught herself wanting to rush away rather than stopping for a chat with teachers and other parents as she had been used to. She was wondering how much the other parents knew about the investigation and what they might be thinking of her. She felt inadequate as a parent and had been wondering what more she could have done to keep Harry out of trouble.

In short, in addition to experiencing a range of intense and negative emotional responses to the school's actions, Linda felt compelled to change her daily routines and to reduce the frequency of her interactions with the children, parents and teachers in Harry's school. Uncertainty about her future career as a swimming coach and negative judgements—made by herself, and assumed to have been made by others—about her personal qualities and character occupied her thoughts on a regular basis.

Kate and a few of her colleagues felt very upset about being sidelined, and about their professional judgement and arguments being ignored during the process of responding to this event. Their loyalty to the school was undermined and they lost some of their respect, not only for Sue, but also for other members of the senior management team. They became uncertain about what topics they could raise during staff meetings and how honest they could be when voicing their opinions about an issue. They felt they had to be constantly on guard during professional discussions in order to avoid major disagreements with Sue. They feared that any difference of opinion could invite a negative response, although they were uncertain what exactly it might be.

Kate became withdrawn during staff discussions and restricted her contributions to an absolute minimum. When she participated, she carefully censored the content of her arguments so as not to antagonise any members of the senior management team. She engaged less freely and less frequently in casual one-to-one conversations with colleagues, as she was not sure any more whom she could trust. Kate felt her professional competence was less frequently recognised and validated by senior staff than before. She became hesitant, both in her classroom and in the playground, when she had to make decisions about what strategy to use in response to behaviour problems. She believed the children must have noticed her momentary uncertainties and felt some of them had become less willing to follow her instructions.

Harry was mostly confused about his teachers' altered responses to him, but he also noticed his mother's distress. He was unable to enjoy his play as much as he used to, as some of his energies were used up constantly trying to please the duty teachers.

This list of the various effects of the decision to qualify the children's pants-pulling as sexual harassment in no way exhausts all the possible effects on Linda, Kate and Harry. We have not even considered here how others—for example, Harry's brother, grandmother and other teachers in the school—might also have been affected. In summary, Linda, Kate and Harry each felt hurt, angry, frustrated or confused. The frequency of their preferred ways of engaging with others was reduced, and some of their usual practices were changed or given up completely. Linda and Kate also started to doubt both their own competence and the beneficence of some others' intentions.

These effects were not just the products of Linda's or Kate's imagination or abstract thinking. They were embodied; that is, they were experienced and felt by them on an ongoing basis. The interruptions were imposed rather than self-initiated changes to their habitual ways of doing and being. In the course of our daily practices, most of us do not consider that the names and labels that we give to people and events might have such gravity.

By going into such detail we wanted to demonstrate how extensive and complex the influence and flow-on effects of one name and one single interpretation of an event can become in people's lives. We hope to have shown that names can invoke different emotional responses, influence the quality of people's relationships with significant others, open and close possibilities for acting in certain ways, and shape the ways people make sense of their identities. Here are the main points.

- The meanings that people make of events and the names they subsequently use to refer to them can have a number of long-lasting and real effects on people.
- Not all names and interpretations have the same currency. The names assigned to events by people in positions of power are more likely to be used to inform people's actions and responses. They also carry value judgements about people and practices.
- Names and meanings can be assigned a truth value and treated as facts about persons, rather than as products of particular assumptions about what the speaker values and what she or he considers acceptable.

In this scenario, Sue, her fellow managers and some staff members did not reflect on the potential effects of the term 'sexual harassment'. They did not think through on the school's behalf the chain of actions such a classification of the events might set in motion. Nor did they consider some of the possible implications of those actions on Linda and Harry, or on the teachers of the school. One name was privileged, as opposed to considering several possible names suggested by staff and the likely outcomes those might produce. Little consideration was given to the underlying assumptions that supported the different names and the kinds of relationship practices those assumptions might render as morally superior. Neither did the staff clarify together the extent to which those assumptions represented the values and teaching philosophy of the teachers in the school.

The problem of inappropriate behaviours was addressed in an individualistic rather than a relational way, with a focus on one child, Harry, rather than on the complexity of interactions that happen in a school. Harry was repeatedly positioned as a problem student rather than being acknowledged as an acceptable one. Further, the assumptions that supported the claim that the children were engaging in 'sexual harassment' were not identified and made open to challenge. Neither were other socially available ideas about children's sexuality discussed by staff. Therefore the teachers did not have an opportunity to clarify what different members of the staff considered 'normal' or 'abnormal' sexual behaviours for children of this age and what, in their view, warranted intervention.

In the following section we present some theoretical concepts that explain more fully why names can have far-reaching consequences. The same concepts can also support a greater awareness of the potentially harmful effects of how people are spoken about and responded to.

Analysis of Harry's story

Harry's story demonstrates how meanings and names can mark out the trajectories of the actions that people will follow. They enable some practices while restraining or disabling others. It does matter whose interpretation of a situation becomes accepted, or, in the absence of consensus, becomes imposed on the situation, as happened for Harry and his peers. The names and labels that are conferred by persons in positions of authority are usually more likely to inform the identity stories that are repeatedly circulated about a person in a school, whether it is a child or a teacher. Others are almost obliged to adopt these names.

Often names of pathological categories dominate these identity stories, excluding other possible perspectives. The ways people, events, actions and behaviours are interpreted and classified thus produce and reproduce power relationships between persons. In this scenario the participants were differently located in the school's social hierarchy. Sue's meaning was privileged as a result of her valued status as deputy principal. Linda's categorisation as a single parent and Kate's categorisation as a beginning teacher did not have the same degree of influence, because those categories did not enjoy similar recognition. It is not too far fetched to conclude that those who are located in less socially valued categories in a particular school community might find it exceptionally difficult to achieve recognition as a good parent, good student or competent teacher. We elaborate on these points below.

What we say matters

In the relationship-centred approach we are proposing, the persons we are and our identities in others' eyes are understood as produced in relationships. We cannot take up particular identities on our own as completely autonomous individuals because we share in the language games that render such identities intelligible. Moreover, meanings and names are a central tool in the relational process of identity production. They are productive and constitutive of possibilities. Davies (2008) argues that a name given to an event or a person is not merely descriptive, "but it provides the terms through which [a person] is *recognised and made recognisable*" (p. 180, italics in original) within the normative order created by that name. Naming the pants-pulling as sexual harassment creates a normative context in which children's exposing of a usually hidden body part becomes something to be concerned about and something to be prevented from happening.

At the same time, the student who participates in such an activity, Harry, becomes recognised and recognisable as someone deviant from the norm for average 6-year-olds. He is seen now as a student who might potentially pose a risk to other students and thus should be subjected to extra supervision. Linda is recognised as an inadequate parent who is also suspected of inappropriate activities.

Linda and Harry have little influence over the choice of the names used by Sue to describe them. Further, Sue's naming is not a one-off, contained event. The term 'sexual harassment' triggers a range of subsequent interventions. In the conversations that follow, particular identities are assigned to both of them. However, the identity assigned to Harry as a perpetrator of sexual harassment is a "thin description" (Geertz, 1983), which could have been thickened with a little more enquiry. Although Linda might think of herself as a caring and devoted parent, and Harry might believe he is no different from other 6-year-olds, they are both socially and relationally constituted differently (Butler, 1997, 2004a), with no reference to their perceptions of themselves by the name selected by Sue and by the ways they are repeatedly spoken about.

Drewery (2005) argues that the process of conversation and the kind of conversational moves people use in response to and about others constitute people's identities in ways they are required to subsequently perform. They thus define not only how we become particular persons and not others, but also the identities that we can take up. She further proposes that it is important to distinguish between *colonising* and respectful ways of speaking, because they have very different effects. Colonising ways of speaking produce relationships in which the meanings of one are hidden and/or not understood. The outcome of this is to subsume the meanings of the one into the meanings of the other. Selves or identities produced in such a way are already inscribed by the meanings of those who determine, without the offer to negotiate, the terms for continuing in conversation. Such interactions, therefore, produce subjugated subjects. (Drewery, 2005, pp. 311–312)

In our scenario, Sue can be said to have engaged in colonising ways of speaking because she was not interested in finding out—and did not offer to negotiate—the meanings Linda or Kate or Harry attributed to the pants-pulling incident. By taking up an authoritarian position, she excluded "the possibility of getting information that might be pertinent" (Drewey, 2005, p. 312) and of which she had no prior knowledge. We can also say that Sue did not offer *speaking positions* (Davies, 1991) to Linda, Harry or Kate from which they could have accounted for their actions and could have explained why they had acted in the ways they did. We will return to the notion of speaking positions shortly.

Repetitive citations and moral orders

The various conversations that others had about Harry and Linda in the staffroom can be considered what Davies (2008) calls "ongoing repetitive citations". Such citations or citational chains work to simultaneously assign particular identities to persons and to confirm a particular moral order. In this case, the staffroom conversations were implicitly informed by the moral judgements of the speakers, which separated the actions of 6-year-olds considered deviant from actions considered normal. This, in turn, positioned those spoken about as "undesirable subjects" (Saltmarsh & Youdell, 2004). Linda was seen as a suspected abusive parent and Harry as both victim of the same abuse but also as a risk to other children. The chosen interventions focused on removing potential risks by segregating Harry from his family or intensifying surveillance on him at school so that he could be separated from other children if he were to threaten their safety.

The process of constituting and reconstituting moral orders provides some persons with what American philosopher Judith Butler (1997) calls a viable existence within a given order, while others are denied it. Harry is unrecognisable as a good student within the moral order that

Sue's actions maintain. It is also impossible to acknowledge Linda as a competent parent within this same regime, because she is the parent of a child who is considered deviant and must bear some responsibility for raising him as such. Kate is engaged in citations that produce a different moral order because she acknowledges Harry as a normal student and rejects Sue's interpretation.

However, her citations, and consequently the order they propose, do not have the same force. Sue's narrative makes reporting Harry to child protection agencies and accusing his family of suspected abuse thinkable and doable and it is her view that becomes dominant. Kate's private conversations with trusted colleagues, however strongly they challenge Sue's repetitions, cannot really rupture or weaken the force of Sue's narrative. Sue speaks in public while Kate's and Linda's interruptions to her speech are carried out in relative secrecy and are not taken seriously by everyone. They cannot, therefore, change the trajectory of the school's and Sue's responses.

Subsequently, Sue's moral order becomes mandatory for all staff. It is her preferred social order that becomes locked "firmly in place", after which "the querying of its moral premises" (Davies, 2008, p. 178) becomes difficult if not impossible. Davies suggests, like Butler (1997), that it is important to provide space for citational practices that interrupt the process of establishing a dominant order in this way. We will come back to explaining further how this can be done under the practice of re-positioning.

Drewery (2005) points out that "[d]ifferent ways of speaking offer different possible effects, and these effects include different possibilities for future actions; these are interactions that are productive of people's lives" (p. 315). In order to demonstrate just how far reaching and life shaping repetitive speech acts can be, we have extracted a few comments made by teachers and have highlighted some of the institutional practices used in response to a 'special sport' class that Sue Saltmarsh and Deborah Youdell (2004) studied in an Australian school. These authors wanted to show how school practices constitute students' and teachers' identities. We think their examples also poignantly bring to life both what Drewery (2005) means by colonising speech and the considerable force of such speech in shaping lives. We hope you get a sense of how the privileging of particular ways of doing and being supports and benefits students who act in those ways but limits the educational opportunities of those who are unable to do so.

The production of undesirable subjects: the 'special sport' class

A male head of department suggested to the researchers that they observe what he called a 'special sport' group. He introduced the class by saying, "I suppose you'd describe these guys as losers of the school" (Saltmarsh & Youdell, 2004, p. 360). He then corrected his description by adding that this group always gets picked on. According to this teacher, the establishment of the special sport class and these students' segregation from other students had been in their best interests because they had been the victims of bullying. The students had failed to effectively respond to ongoing bullying and so their special placement could also be considered a protective measure, in the absence of which they would be truant from sport classes. Other male members of the physical education department also spoke about the same students in a condescending manner, noticed by both the researchers and the female teacher of the class, Ms Sims: "Of course, Mr Pratt doesn't help. Whenever he makes announcements during assembly … he always says, 'And Ms Sims' special sport will meet in the quad'" (p. 361). Ms Sims noted that since Mr Pratt had started referring to the group as "Ms Sims' special sport", other students had felt encouraged to hassle and tease them, and to call them names, such as a "bunch of ignorant wimps".

The majority of the students in the class were classified as having mild intellectual disabilities or a physical disability, but there were also students who were described as competent sportsmen. They had joined this group to be with a disabled sibling, or because they did not have to pay school fees in this class. However, the heterogeneous composition of the group was not mentioned in conversations about the class.

The group was expected to bring their own equipment as the school only provided sports equipment to fee-paying groups. These students were thus trying to play games such as cricket, volleyball, softball and hockey, without the same equipment that was provided to fee-paying students. Subsequently, they would be constituted as undesirable male student subjects in the school's social hierarchy. The student:teacher ratio in this group was twice that of other groups. The teacher, Ms Sims, had been stopped from coaching prestigious games, such as cricket, because she had an allergy to deodorants, which prevented her from being able to accompany students on the bus. When students deliberately sprayed deodorants on her, senior managers did nothing about it. Saltmarsh and Youdell (2004) note that the

> derogatory terminology deployed in descriptions of the group, together with persistent omission of other pertinent information about the class and the students in it, reflects the extent to which this group functions as a repository for the school's hopeless cases. (p. 363)

The absence of concern for her health also placed Ms Sims, like her students, low in the school's institutional hierarchy. The positioning of the group as having low status and worth was further confirmed by how spaces were allocated to them. The group had to play in the quad, which was a concreted area "flanked by the caged canteen on one side and the classroom buildings with walls of windows on the other three sides" (p. 366). When students tried to play cricket or soccer there, they not only had to put up with the reflection of heat and glare from the sun, but they also had to restrict their movements so that they would not break any windows. If they did, then they would have to pay repair costs. While other groups used purpose-built facilities, the allocation of the concrete quad to this group further reinforced their subordinate position.

Saltmarsh and Youdell powerfully demonstrate not only how the naming practices employed in a particular school can constitute some students as "outside acceptable social, sporting or educational masculinities" (p. 370). They also describe how the process of repetitive citations works:

> The title given to the class, its particular staffing allocation, the apparent absence of material resources and the nature of the space allocated to the group can all be understood as institutional practices of educational triage that severely limit the educational opportunities of this group of students. (p. 370)

By categorising students according to their sporting abilities and dividing them up into different classes, the school establishes its own norm of what types of persons it considers desirable and undesirable. We can see from the above example that once the students are allocated to different groups they will perform different activities, which in turn will develop their skills differently. Some students will have more time and resources invested in them, so that they can be trained to become the kind of students the school seems to privilege: students with sporting bodies who could win competitions and contribute to the reputation of the school. Those who are assessed to have less potential will not receive the same attention and training. They are in a way excess to requirements, or, as Foucault (1980) argues, they are exposed as redundant and as such "banned, excluded and repressed" (p. 100).

The systems of the school and the practices employed on a daily basis are thus geared to support the skill development of those students who fit the normative ideal of the school. The same practices work differently on those who are less talented in sport. They actually restrict, rather than support, the development of these students' competencies. Behaviour management and disciplinary practices in schools operate in a similar manner: they also work to produce ideal student subjects, who behave as expected and have skills that are valued.

Harry noticed the extra surveillance used on him during intervals. In turn, this conscious awareness made him regulate his own conduct and body by changing his usual pattern of play. He moved around more cautiously and interrupted his play by frequently checking to see whether his teachers' body language could be read as approval of what he was doing, or not doing. Here we want to demonstrate that when difference from the norm is treated as both problematic and morally inferior, the school's systems and practices can be used to act "upon the actions" (Foucault, 1982, p. 220) of students, keeping some in their places at the bottom of the hierarchy and turning others into ideal and desirable subjects.

Difference and recognition

To be recognised as 'proper', 'ideal' or 'good' is important for all of us. In schools, students want recognition as good students and teachers want to be considered effective teachers. Rewards and awards are "mechanisms of recognising individuals who have excelled or performed in excess of the norm" (Davies et al., 2013). Children are often presented with certificates or other more or less tangible forms of reward, such as stickers, a pencil, a book or free time. The achievement of higher overall scores on tests or sustained compliance with school rules can also earn acknowledgement.

Davies et al. (2013) note that, while recognition might affirm individual differences in performance, especially when persons perform better than others, it also encourages conformity and compliance with norms. Recognition, therefore, is also a mechanism of regulation and control, often used in concert with punishment. Excellent performances of the norm are rewarded, while poor and below-average performances might be punished with corrective or protective interventions, as was the case for Harry. Most people want recognition rather than punishment. They will, therefore, behave in ways that conform to normative standards, whatever those might be in a particular context.

Students are no different. The majority of them will aspire to fit within categories of normality rather than stand out as different. However, this might be easier said than done. Often a person's own efforts to act according to the prescriptions of a given standard might not be enough to earn validation as a good or acceptable person. Behaviours are also subjected to value judgements made by both others and by ourselves. Harry and the other children probably did not want to be seen as naughty and thus outside the category of good student. According to their own evaluation of their behaviour, pants-pulling was an acceptable act. Sue, on the other hand, pronounced them as outside the category of good student and her ruling carried more weight than the children's interpretation. The process of recognition, as with repetitive citations, demonstrates that our individual identities depend on relationships.

Vulnerability to others and viable lives

Judith Butler (2004b) proposes that our humanity and very existence rely on recognition. Those who are repeatedly recognised as falling within normative and socially valued categories can have a viable life. Those who are repeatedly seen to fall short become abject 'Others', who are relegated to the group of undesirable and often invisible subjects. Butler uses as an example public obituaries in relation to extreme events, such as the loss of human lives in wars, or in terrorist attacks like the events of 9/11. She notes that after such events conflicting groups would mourn and recognise as tragic losses their own members, while the innocent casualties, such as children and women, among the members of the other group might not be mentioned at all by the media. In addition, the behaviours and personal characteristics of those considered worthy of recognition are usually praised and spoken about as something to aspire to. The behaviours and characteristics of those deemed 'Other', on the other hand, only get a mention as a reminder of what persons should refrain from if they want to fit in and do well.

What has all this got to do with schools, and with Harry in our scenario? Schools also have a range of public practices of recognition, such as the handing out of certificates at whole-school assemblies in acknowledgement of sustained excellent performance or compliance with the school's rules and norms. Good citizenship awards honour those who follow instructions and do not break school rules. Some schools—fortunately not many—might also create public forums for naming and shaming those who have transgressed rules.

Practices of recognition can establish degrees of worthiness in the institutional hierarchy in a manner similar to how the previously described repetitive iterations, and ways of speaking and responding to particular students can divide a school's population into desirable and undesirable subjects. Leach and Lewis (2013) provide examples of how circles, a strategy of community building, can be transformed by some teachers into shaming individuals and making them listen to advice from the rest of the class. Harry could easily have been on the receiving end of such advice giving.

Decisions about which differences are socially more valued than others and which are rejected are not always clear cut. Shildrick (2000, 2007) has written about the differential social and moral value attached to variations in the physical characteristics of the human body. She has shown how idealised bodies, like the ones portrayed by ancient Greek and Roman statues, mark out the bodies of people with disabilities as deficient and repugnant, while also making them objects of voyeurism. Shildrick argues that the boundaries of categories—of the ideal and normal and of the 'Other'—cannot be fixed and held in place indefinitely. We all fit some notions of the normal or ideal but in some situations we might be judged 'Other'. The boundaries of categories are usually leaky and permeable, depending on the moral values held by those who do the categorising.

Harry's behaviours were judged to be both normal and problematic by two different teachers because they each subscribed to different assumptions about child behaviours. According to Butler (2004b), this shows our vulnerability to others, because they decide whether our differences are accepted or not, and she also points out the ethical responsibility that such vulnerability calls for. It is not only recognition of worthiness that we should be issuing to others who are different: we should also acknowledge that "[w]e are all, in different ways, striving for recognition" (p. 44) and that vulnerability exists as the "precondition for humanisation" (p. 43).

Butler and Shildrick both emphasise the importance of relationality, which we also want to demonstrate in this book. We are not separate individuals but need others to become who we want to be. Harry cannot be left to his own devices to become a good student on his own. He has to be recognised and validated as such by others—his teachers and his peers. In Chapters 3 and 4 we will return to how it is possible to produce students as desirable rather than undesirable subjects.

The ideology of normal

The example of the special sport class demonstrates that schools can establish their own norms regarding what they consider acceptable and unacceptable behaviours, achievements and appearances, along with what differences they will tolerate or sanction. Annamma, Boelé, Moore and Klingner (2013) suggest that notions of normal are often constructed by idealising the average as good and something to be desired. The idealisation of the average is based on and supported by the Gaussian bell-shaped curve, a statistical measurement tool of achievement, which "promotes the notion that some students will excel, most will be average, and some will fail" (p. 1278). Such division of the student population creates a hierarchy, in which the average is more socially valued than any differences from it. The average thus becomes the norm and the ideal that everyone should aspire to. This makes any difference from the norm or average problematic, while the notion of normal becomes common sense: 'the way we do things here'. Davies (2013) suggests that problems can arise when "the way things are comes to be what is expected, and the expected slides quickly into morality:

is becomes *ought*. The normative becomes the socially approved way of being" (p. 21).

Within this framework, uniformity and conformity to standards are privileged, while the variability and diversity of humans are disregarded. Differences are scrutinised in order to establish their tolerability, but whatever is considered common sense will be unavailable for reflection. "When normal is held as the standard, our systems and structures impose oppressive practices on deviance from the norm" (Annamma et al., 2013, p. 1283).

There are numerous examples internationally of various oppressive, punitive and discriminatory practices that school systems employ in response to those students who are seen to deviate from the norm. In most English-speaking countries, students of colour and students from different ethnic minorities are disproportionately represented in statistics of underachievement.

In New Zealand, the Te Kotahitanga programme put this issue on the agenda of educators. It also successfully addressed the differential achievement of Māori students (Bishop, Berryman, Cavanagh, & Teddy, 2007). Test results improved significantly in schools where teachers used more culturally responsive pedagogies (Bishop & Berryman, 2006). In the US, students from minority groups are more likely to be selected for special education. Students of colour who have the same disability as their white peers are more likely to be placed in segregated rather than mainstream classrooms (Sullivan, 2011). Minority students have been shown to be the target of punitive disciplinary measures, such as stand-downs and suspensions, more frequently than their white peers (Noguera, 2003; Skiba et al., 2002). Though stand-down and suspension rates for Māori and Pasifika students are improving in New Zealand, they are still higher than those for New Zealand European or Asian students (Ministry of Education, 2010). Annamma et al. (2013) suggest that such disparities can be the product of narrow definitions of 'normal'. It is not the students who need to change but the notion of normal that has to be widened, and human diversity and variability should be accepted as the norm. In the last section of this chapter we will introduce a relationship practice that we think can support teachers with accommodating difference by 'loosening the grip of normal'.

Loosening the grip of normal

Categories are not always negative or harmful. We rely on them for our very existence as we take up our identities from pre-existing categories (Davies, 2006). Familiar labels and names can provide safety and a shared understanding of behaviours, events, persons and phenomena, saving us from the obligation to repeatedly explain ourselves as we engage in conversations with others.

Categories become problematic when their meanings become fixed and they are used as "methods of observation, techniques of registration, procedures for investigation and research, apparatuses of control" (Foucault, 1980, p. 102). They will then keep people in their places and prevent change, because they can be used to repeatedly validate and maintain the same order with the same power relationships, benefiting some but disadvantaging others. It can be psychologically and emotionally very burdensome if a person is locked out of categories of normality on an ongoing basis. Permanent social exclusion not only produces destructive emotional responses but can be injurious to a person's identity work as well, because it can invite strong feelings of self-doubt. Identity work can be thought of as the ongoing process of constructing a personal identity by interacting with and internalising socially recognised categories of identity.

In order to provide recognition for everyone, first we have to acknowledge that the boundaries of categories are not fixed, but flexible. It is always possible to stretch them if we are ready and willing to revise and renegotiate their meanings. Sue and Kate had very different interpretations of the pants-pulling. What they did not have is a conversation about their respective interpretations, which might have been able to destabilise the term 'sexual harassment'.

Second, as Davies (2008) suggests, we have to take responsibility not only for our intentions but also for the effects of all repetitive citations that we engage in, because they can potentially render people's lives unviable. It has to be noted that without the repetitious implementation of systems, structures and practices, teachers and students might find it difficult to get on with the job of teaching and learning. A well-established system that everyone is familiar with can be satisfying, because it ensures the smooth operation of a place. However, we concur with Davies (2008), who calls for:

> a reflexive examination of how that which grants one pleasure and security and power may be harming others, withholding from them the possibility of viable life. The 'behaviour' that needs rethinking in arenas of conflict, both in schools and elsewhere, is the citational production of the un-reflected ordinary world. (p. 185)

Sue did not reflect on her practices, or on what kind of school she was producing as ordinary.

Positioning theory

So far this chapter has referred to colonising speech, repeated citations of the normative order, categorising and normalising, and providing or withholding recognition of difference, all of which can contribute to the production of desirable or undesirable subjects. All of these are also relationship practices and mechanisms through which we position ourselves and others in relationships. The notion of positioning can help us understand the productive power of conversations and how we might be complicit in contributing to and maintaining injustice (Davies, 2008; Davies & Harré, 1990; Drewery, 2005; Winslade, 2005).

Positioning also helps us recognise that not all utterances and conversations have the same force. Those in positions of authority or those who repeatedly affirm the existing ordinary world or the moral order that enjoys institutional support can do so without much effort. According to positioning theory (Davies & Harré, 1990), as we open our mouths and speak, we inevitably take up positions and accord others positions from which we expect them to respond. Each utterance implicitly establishes a moral order, at least temporarily. There is often a fluidity about this, because people can shift their positions from one utterance to another. Deleuze and Guattari (1987) might refer to the presence of such fluidity as more "smooth spaces" (p. 474). On the other hand, there are also over-determined patterns of repetition that lead to positions being established as norms. These positions are like wheel ruts on a dirt road. They are hard to avoid or to get out of. Deleuze and Guattari might call them more "striated spaces" (p. 474). Each utterance sets up a relationship in a particular format.

When Sue used the term 'sexual harassment', for example, she set up a narrow range of positions from which Harry and Linda could respond. He was now positioned as a perpetrator and his utterances would be understood from this position, while Linda was positioned as an inadequate parent. They could refuse these positions, but to do so has dangers and may risk being positioned in more catastrophic or even more highly striated places.

Davies (2008) argues that citations of the dominant order are always easier to perform than what she calls "rebellious speech". The latter is more risky because it interrupts and challenges dominant views. It can, therefore, also have negative existential consequences for those who engage in it. Sue could carry on as usual with her preferred world views, while Kate reduced and censored her contributions to staff discussions and only shared her opinions with trusted colleagues. In the remainder of this chapter we nevertheless provide examples of how it is possible to rethink, revise and challenge "the citational production of the un-reflected ordinary world" (Davies, 2008, p. 185)

Speaking and silent positions

Davies (2008, p. 182) shows two different positionings of a student called Shane: one by Bob, a principal of a regular school, and the other by Cath, the principal of a special school for students who struggle to overcome behaviour problems. Shane was in the process of being reintegrated into Bob's regular school and he attended a school assembly there wearing a baseball cap. Bob instructed Shane to take his hat off but he did not move.

After a repeat command from Bob to remove his hat, Shane walked out of assembly. Bob responded, "Stay right there. Don't turn your back on me, son! Come back here right now!" He subsequently suspended Shane for 2 days. When Shane was brought back to the special school by his mother, Cath, the principal of that school asked him what happened. Shane told her that he would not take his hat off.

When Cath said, "Good heavens—you made that your hill to die on?", Shane removed his hat and revealed a patchily bald, bad haircut. He added, "I couldn't take it off and let everyone see this!"

Cath replied, "No, I guess not."

The difference between these two interactions is significant. Cath offered Shane a speaking position (Davies, 1990, 1991), from which he could account for himself and explain why he could not remove the cap in front of the whole school. She was open to entertaining other possibilities than the one presented by Bob, which read Shane's walk-out as disobedience. She was interested in finding out other relevant information that might have been left out of the conversation but could be pertinent.

Cath did not impose her meaning on the situation, leaving space for Shane to enter information into the conversational exchange that provided a reasonable explanation for his actions and that also positioned him as 'normal' rather than deviant. This piece of information, about the bad haircut, had to remain hidden in Shane's exchange with Bob, who positioned Shane as a silent spectator (Drewery, 2005) who could not influence in any way the decision made about him at that moment. Cath, on the other hand, was open to examining and revising the habituated citations employed in schools, which would only allow her to read a student's non-compliance as disobedience and position the student outside the category of normal as an undesirable school subject.

The practice of (re-)positioning

Cath showed, in another exchange with 11-year-old Robert, that alternative positions can also be found even in potentially dangerous and serious situations (Laws & Davies, 2000, p. 218). Robert, another student in Cath's special school, climbed up onto the roof of the school building as a protest against some injustice that he believed had happened to his friend. He threatened to burn the school down and shouted that he hated everyone. When Cath tried to warn him about the slippery roof, Robert responded with swear words: "Get fucked. You are all bastards."

Cath considered whether she should ask what had happened, enter negotiations or talk about consequences and wise choices. She reflected instead on the discourse in which he was operating and said, "I didn't know this about you. I didn't know that you had such a strong sense of justice and will do just about anything if you thought a friend had been wronged."

Robert came down from the roof and spent the rest of the afternoon doing work in his classroom.

In this exchange Cath again managed to go beyond the readily available, usual notions of schooling and offered Robert a position as protester against injustice rather than the position of delinquent student. She attributed a different meaning to his actions from the ones that the habitual citations and stories of schooling made available. She *positioned* or *re-positioned* Robert outside the usual teacher–student relationship by reading his actions as a stand against injustice rather than as non-compliance. She could have asserted her view or knowledge of what had happened, and she had the choice of calling Robert's parents, her colleagues or even the police. Instead, she worked to position both Robert and herself in speaking, rather than silent, positions, which invited collaboration from Robert rather than further resistance. This story demonstrates how the power of the teacher can be used to help students reach beyond undesirable subject positions and also beyond the positions offered to them through unexamined and un-reflected repetitive citations.

Sue could have re-positioned Harry in a similar manner. She could have asked the children what name they would have given to their pants-pulling game. She could also have told them, "Pulling down pants is a rather silly game. Remember our school rule about respecting other people's space and belongings. What other funny games do you think you could play that won't get you into trouble?" Such a response would have positioned the children not as deviant or delinquent but as young persons who are in the process of learning about what behaviours are accepted in their school and thus allowed to make mistakes. They would have been positioned as still needing reminders and adult support. Asking the children what other games they could think of would have offered them a speaking position from which they could have demonstrated that they were capable of making decisions and correcting mistakes.

Summary of main points in Chapter 2

- Teachers' utterances carry with them the authority of their role.
- The extent to which they carry authority is related to the teacher's position in the school hierarchy.
- Citational practices are those in which people are named as a desirable or undesirable category of person.
- These naming practices can be abusive of students, even when they are not intended to be.
- They are most likely to be abusive when they consign students to positions that are not viable and that do not have speaking rights.

- They are usually justified with reference to the need to maintain order.
- It can be risky to rebel against the ways you have been named.
- Teachers can, however, avoid using colonising language practices.
- They can welcome 'rebellious' acts not so much as threats but as openings to lines of flight.
- They can re-position students in speaking positions and as protagonists in their own stories.
- They can be curious about new knowledge or new insights they might learn from students.
- They can treat students as worthy of respect with valuable contributions to offer.

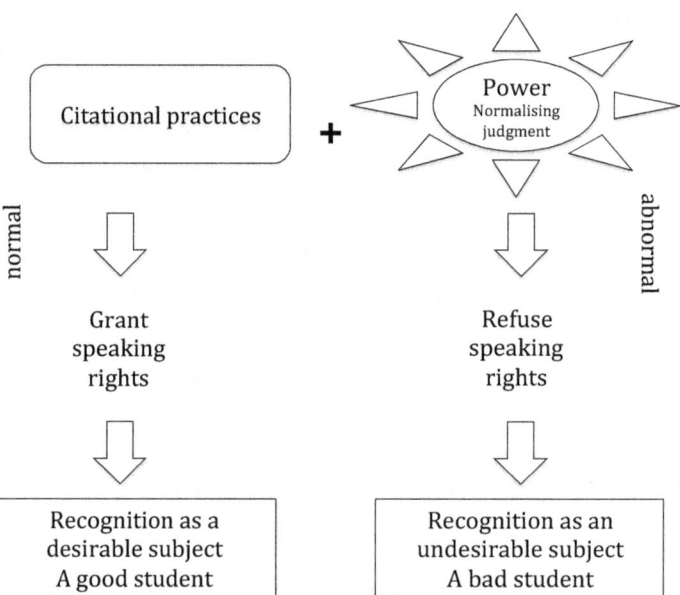

Figure 2: Citational practices

Exercise

You are a teacher in a (secondary) school and some students in the classroom respond to your instructions by shrugging their shoulders, making faces and overtly displaying their reluctance to get their books out. When, after repeated requests to do their work, you tell them this is learning time, one of them says, "So?"

Choose a name from the list that you think best describes this response. Do you consider it to be:
- disobedience
- protest against some injustice
- something else?

Now consider the effects of your choice by discussing your answers to the following questions with a colleague:
- What line of action becomes available to the teacher, the student (or others involved) if you describe the event by this name?
- What kind of intervention will you follow?
- What kind of relationships between teacher and student, teacher and parents, teacher and other students, and student and other students become available to you if you name the event this way?

Repeat this activity by reflecting on two different names that were given to the same events, persons or behaviours in relation to a situation you can recall. In addition to answering the previous questions, consider the following:
- Whose name had more influence / was accepted by most people? Why do you think this was so?
- Who was offered speaking positions and who was silenced?
- What differences were recognised and what differences were undesirable?

Questions for reflection

1. Can you think of times when the way you were spoken about—the repetitive citations used about you—limited or could have limited your educational opportunities?
2. When have you felt you were not offered a speaking position?
3. What were the effects of such ways of speaking on you or on your actions?
4. How did this situation affect your relationships with others?

Chapter 3 The stance of curiosity: "Don't lie to me. You were stalking her"

Introduction

The previous chapter focused on how moral judgements about persons' differences can turn them into undesirable subjects, and how the withholding or selective provision of recognition can have disabling effects on students' educational opportunities. This chapter shifts attention to how the validation or rejection of persons' knowledges—what they think about issues, events and people, and what they tell about their own experiences—can determine whether they become seen as problematic or acceptable subjects.

Acceptance of and respect for differences often ride on how people relate to *knowledges*, or the stories that tell how the world should be. If a particular knowledge or story is seen to represent a fixed truth, because it is believed to reflect how things are 'out there' in the world, then stories that convey a different version of events can be rejected, silenced or discarded completely.

Such conceptualisations of knowledge propose their own version of how things work, why people behave in certain ways and not others, how children learn and how people could overcome problems, among other things. Evidence or proof plays an important role in legitimising claims to truth within this approach.

Other, mainly postmodern approaches, argue that it is not possible to represent exactly an undistorted or 'mirror image' of the world and of how things are. In the human sciences, particularly, what we claim to know about things and people, therefore, cannot be fixed. We all interpret and make different meanings of the same event or action, as was shown in Chapter 1.

In this chapter we consider the different relational outcomes produced when relationship practices are informed by either of these two different approaches to knowledge. It is easier to persuade teachers in schools to apply the first approach, what we have termed 'the stance of certainty', because teachers' work also includes the transfer of a body of knowledge accumulated over time in the disciplines they teach, such as maths, physics, biology, history and psychology. Teachers have to operate from a position of certainty when they explain new concepts and ideas. However, we also suggest that such a stance of certainty, while useful when teaching new content, can also exacerbate, rather than resolve, relationship conflict. We introduce the principles of what we have called 'the stance of curiosity', based on Anderson and Goolishian's (1992) description of a particular approach to the stories people tell about their lives. We show how such an approach can be more productive, especially in conflict situations and when teachers perform their pastoral care duties.

Who is telling the truth?: Andrew's dilemma

Andrew, a dean in a secondary school, received a complaint from Anna about John. She claimed that John had been stalking her. John and Anna were in the same form class but their teachers thought they belonged to different cliques and had little to do with one another. Both students were on the periphery of their teachers' awareness as neither had been at the receiving end of disciplinary procedures before. Andrew had had one previous encounter with John, when, some months previously John had been the target of bullying and had been repeatedly called a 'faggot' by some boys. The bullying students used John's feminine looks and his friendship with girls as a justification for their actions. Andrew had dealt successfully with the bullies then and had not heard from John since. He was somewhat surprised that, on this occasion, John was accused of perpetrating bullying.

Andrew took his pastoral care duties very seriously and tried to follow up any complaints on the same day they were received if his other commitments allowed. Students said to be involved in a conflict were invited to his office for a conversation. At the time of Anna's complaint about John, Andrew was participating in ongoing professional development and was learning to use restorative conversations in his work. He had been introduced to the concept of positioning during a workshop, where the facilitator had given examples of how a person's category membership might position them differently, more favourably or less favourably, in the social hierarchy.

Andrew was particularly interested in relationships of power relating to gender. He often had conversations with colleagues about how being a male might more easily afford a teacher respect from students without having to 'work for it' as hard as he believed his female colleagues had to. Andrew did not want such undeserved respect, so he tried hard to gain the respect of his students through acting fairly and consistently. He tried to avoid using his strong voice and position as a male member of the senior management team to invoke fear. He took care to be as gentle as possible, especially when he interviewed girls. Therefore, Andrew's first response was to listen with sympathy to Anna, and to express his dismay about John's behaviours towards her. He reassured her that he was going to follow up the matter with John.

Immediately after listening to Anna, Andrew called John to his office. He confronted him in an accusatory tone of voice and told him that he was really disappointed in his "appalling attitude to women". John was, at first, so shocked that he was unable to say anything in his own defence. When he managed to pull himself together a few minutes later he vehemently denied the stalking allegations.

Andrew responded, "Don't lie to me. She told me that you were stalking her."

John was convinced that Andrew's negative reaction could only be brought about by Andrew's limited knowledge of his relationship with Anna. Had Andrew been privy to some other, pertinent information that must have been left out of Anna's story, he would have drawn different conclusions. In particular, John thought it would be important for Andrew to know about an argument that he had recently had with Anna, during which Anna had threatened him with revenge if he failed to send derogatory text messages to one of her friends as proof of his loyalty to her. John refused, as he believed such messages would constitute bullying. He had not wanted to get into trouble either. He thought the accusation of stalking must have been Anna's revenge, but he was given no chance to tell his side of the story. He left the deans' office distressed, so much so that he could not pay attention during the following lesson. He found it really difficult to stop himself from crying.

Marian, a teacher's assistant, noticed John's distress and asked him what the matter was. She had a good relationship with John and had known him and his family reasonably well since he was a baby. John told her what he had been accused of doing but insisted that Anna had lied to the dean as revenge for his refusal to carry out text bullying on her behalf. Marian was a quiet but permanent presence in the class and she regularly offered to help students with their work, in addition to the support she provided for two special needs students. She spent more time with the whole class than any teacher as she accompanied them to every lesson. She was, therefore, able to witness student interactions and she overheard conversations that remained unknown to the teachers who taught the class. Marian was also considered to be a grandmother figure by the students and they often used her as a confidante. She certainly believed that John's relationship with Anna was complicated and the stalking allegations might only be part of the full story.

The whole situation and seeing John's pain really upset Marian. Considering the information she had about John's and Anna's relationship, she thought that it would constitute a miscarriage of justice if Andrew failed to investigate further and gather more information before deciding on a punishment. John could have been stood down for a few days, which could set off a number of unwanted consequences at home.

Marian also had information about John's mental health that nobody else at the school was privy to. John had told her that he had struggled with depression before, so Marian was worried that an injustice like the accusation could trigger a relapse. She knew that John's parents were very strict and they would believe the dean rather than him. As a consequence they would be likely to remove some of his privileges, such as the use of his mobile phone or permitting him to go out with friends in weekends. They had done so on previous occasions. She suspected that John's visible distress was not only triggered by the relationship problems with Anna but also by being scared of his parents.

Marian was aware that John and Anna had been friends for a few months. In her opinion John was the one who was trying to please Anna most of the time, and not the other way round. Other students in the class commented on this power dynamic in a disapproving manner to Marian. They found it difficult to accept that John seemed to agree with everything Anna decided and that he seldom challenged her. In their opinion, John was so desperate to have a girlfriend that he was willing to put up with unfair treatment. Even Anna had admitted to Marian that she had been "wearing the pants" in her relationship with John.

Anna had also told Marian how angry she had been with John because he would not do as she asked. She had confessed that, in a moment of feeling upset, she had decided to tell on him to the dean. Seeing John's distress, she regretted her actions but was scared to go back to the dean for fear of being called a liar. Andrew had a reputation as a teacher who detested uncertainties and also students who changed their story. He preferred people to stick to their story. A modification was considered by him to be both a lie and a testament to weak character.

Marian reluctantly offered to mediate in the matter. She felt that, as a teacher aide, she would not be welcome to intervene in disciplinary matters. She requested another appointment for both John and Anna from Andrew but all three of them were uncertain whether Andrew would be willing to grant one more opportunity. In the end he did, and we will relate how that meeting went when we return to this story later in the chapter.

What can we make of this complex friendship problem?

Andrew decided to treat one version of the events, Anna's, as fact and he left no space for any other alternatives. His practice was informed by the assumption that students either tell the truth or they lie. Within this logic there can only be one correct story. Once the 'true' representation of the facts is identified, any other account of what happened should be disqualified as a blatant lie.

After he had made his decision Andrew had no further interest in exploring John's side of the story. He was convinced that there was no need to ask about John's interpretation of what had happened. He believed the first version of the story as presented to him by Anna. He did not think it necessary to listen to and explore any other alternatives—John's or those of witnesses who might have been around Anna and John when the alleged stalking took place. Andrew trusted his capacity to separate fact from fiction based on minimal information, so he did not see a need to take the matter further. By quickly assigning fixed identities to John and Anna, that of stalker to him and that of victim to her, he shut down rather than opened up possibilities. He affirmed, and presented as truth, what he thought he knew. He was not willing to entertain, or seek out, a less obvious, more surprising or unexpected account of the events that had taken place. He was not willing to revise his initial interpretation of the events.

We can also say that Andrew acted in a manner that is the dominant mode of engagement between teachers and students in schools. He took up a position of knowing or expertise, and was certain that his decision did not need revising. In spite of the ready availability of pedagogies that encourage teachers to give up their expert position and to co-construct knowledge with their students, the organisation of school life is such that most teachers have to operate from such a position of expert a lot of the time. For example, when teachers explain new concepts, demonstrate the applications of a mathematical formula, set up a laboratory experiment and prepare resources, among other things, they have to convince their students that they know what they are talking about. If they came across as hesitant or unsure about a definition or the meaning of a word, their students might not take them seriously and they would find it difficult to teach. If teachers continually challenged and tried to revise the very concepts, ideas, mathematical formulas, historical accounts and so on, the job of teaching would become incredibly hard, if not impossible. In addition, teachers are also expected to lead and make quick decisions on the spot about what should happen next. There is no time to negotiate every decision.

We suggest that such positioning of a teacher as 'the knower' is not so helpful when teachers try to resolve conflict or to build relationships with students. In those situations a more tentative stance might be more productive and might lead to more satisfying outcomes for all involved. Below we will distinguish between taking up an expert position and what we call a 'not-knowing' stance.

Analysis of Andrew's dilemma

Two different approaches to knowledge

Positivist and empiricist traditions in science assume "that the nature of the world can be revealed by observation, and that what exists is what we *perceive* to exist" (Burr, 1995, p. 3, emphasis in original). Knowledge obtained by objective observation, therefore, is trustworthy, because it reflects or mirrors the world. Interpretive or postmodern approaches to knowledge, on the other hand, reject this view and claim that what we call knowledge is a *construction* or a particular version of the world "that has received the stamp of 'truth' in our society" (Burr, 1995, p. 64). Every time we define something, we produce an interpretation of it rather than reflect the objective reality.

This is a simplistic account, but we can say that quantitative and qualitative research paradigms are based on these two different approaches to what counts as knowledge. Quantitative researchers seek out observable and replicable data as evidence. For example, they would decide whether a specific behaviour management or restorative strategy is effective or not by counting and comparing the number of bullying incidents or stand-downs before and after the introduction of an intervention. Qualitative researchers, on the other hand, might interview teachers and students, and their perception of what has changed would be used as evidence.

The first approach claims to know exactly what has or what can be changed, such as the number of bullying incidents. The second approach is more tentative and might identify changes that cannot be measured so easily. It would accept what people believe to have changed and the practices to which they attribute positive effects. For example, in a scenario where the number of bullying incidents has not reduced as a result of an intervention, teachers and students might still claim that the intervention was useful, because they have been able to deal with difficult situations more confidently, which, in turn, has reduced their stress levels. The first approach focuses on a narrow range of predetermined and measurable changes and claims to be able to prove that they have taken place. The second approach might throw up a range of unimagined and surprising perceptions of the changes rather than claiming to deliver unquestionable facts.

Professionals who work in educational contexts, such as teachers, psychologists and therapists, might treat their own expertise or knowledge in similar ways. The quality of their relationships with students and their mode of engagement are going to be very different, depending on the approach they take. If, for example, teachers, school counsellors or psychologists consider their assessments of situations to be correct 'diagnoses', because they reflect how things really are, then it is very likely that they will offer a solution in the manner that doctors prescribe medication and will tell students what to do. They will not be interested in the knowledge students might have about their own lives.

Such privileging of the expert's views has been shown to be detrimental to clients in psychotherapy (Parker, 1999), but we think it can be equally damaging in the school context, especially in situations where conflicts are addressed. This is not to say that professional expertise cannot be helpful. However, John's example shows that further problems can result from ignoring some sources of information. If professionals, like Andrew in our example, would accept that their assessment is only one of many possible interpretations, then they would be willing to take into consideration expertise or knowledge other than their own—such as John's version of events in addition to Anna's. They would also be open to revising and changing a diagnosis.

The issue is not so much about which approach reflects reality better than the other. The issue is whether one is willing to revise interpretations, because one accepts that there can be many possible meanings and no one can be certain of knowing them all. There are therefore dangers that lie in privileging one interpretation over others as the truth.

Some therapists deliberately draw on an interpretive approach to knowledge production when they try to make sense of people's problems. White and Epston (1990), two prominent practitioners of narrative therapy, have applied the notion of interpretation to the stories that people tell about their life experiences, together with the concept of analogies or maps, drawing on Gregory Bateson's work. They claim that when people interpret events, they also select particular analogies or maps and employ these as interpretive frameworks. The maps or frameworks used will then determine how specific events are explained, what kinds of conclusions are drawn, and how people will story their experiences. In other words, the interpretations of any event will be determined by how they fit known patterns: "Those events that cannot be 'patterned' are not selected for survival; such events will not exist for us as facts" (White & Epstein, 1990, p. 2). This also explains why stories are full of gaps and why they might change during a subsequent retelling, as the storyteller increases or reduces the number of events selected for inclusion. The storyteller might also select completely different events, depending on the plot or thematic framework used.

We believe that people apply the same selective process of knowledge production in their personal relationships when they decide what to accept or reject of the stories that others tell them about events. Relationships between teachers and students are no exception. Andrew came up with one possible interpretation of John's story and relied on particular maps about gender relationships. According to one of the maps he used, it was more often males than females who bully, assault or abuse their partners. According to another map that informed his interpretive work, males could more easily take advantage of and use their bodily presence to invoke fear than females. He listened to and selected 'for survival' events that fitted these maps but was unable to consider other possibilities. These interpretive maps thus shaped his response to both Anna and John.

Andrew also tried to avoid the reproduction of a similar power relationship between himself and female students. He worked hard to counterbalance the potential negative effects of his positioning as a male teacher in a management role. He felt he needed to protect girls more than boys. He read John's actions within these frameworks, as opposed to exploring what Anna's contribution might have been. He assumed John's guilt and Anna's innocence. The events that fitted these maps survived and became part of his account, while other events (for example, the possibility that John might have been seeking to please Anna uncritically, and that Anna might blackmail John into compliance with text bullying in exchange for her friendship) could not be heard by him. These possibilities also remained inadmissible into the conversation by John.

Anna had also followed a relationship map, according to which she could legitimately expect compliance with her demands in exchange for her friendship, even when such compliance forced others to act contrary to their values or break the law, or the school rules, as with John. 'Real' friendship, according to this framework, could only be proven through absolute surrender to the other's wishes.

In Anna's story, John's refusal to perform text bullying was read as a breach of the friendship covenant and not as breaking some kind of moral code that rejects psychological harm to others through anonymous texting. She felt justified in punishing the 'traitor' in the friendship by telling on him to the dean. When, after witnessing and realising the negative impact of her actions on John, she regretted her actions, she used another interpretive map, one that condemns hurting friends. But remedying the situation seemed difficult for her, because she did not want to be seen as a liar. Protecting her victim status in Andrew's books was more important to her than putting things right with her friend. And so on.

There is no space here to elaborate on John's interpretive map in more detail, but we will refer to it next, when we discuss the concept of *power/knowledge*. It is possible to see from John's emotional response, however, that it was not his interpretation that received 'the stamp of truth' in this instance. In Chapters 5 and 6 we will return to the notion of knowledge as discourse. In this chapter we will continue to use the term 'knowledge'.

Knowledge production and power/knowledge

The previously described selective and interpretive process of knowledge production also sets up particular power relationships between people because it positions them differently in various social hierarchies. Foucault (1972) claimed the inseparability of power from knowledge and knowledge from power in relation to the scientific disciplines. He observed how these disciplines construct knowledges as "regimes of truth" (Foucault, 1980), and how significant "the production, accumulation, circulation and functioning" (p. 93) of knowledge is for the exercise of power. He stated, "We cannot exercise power except through the production of truth" (p. 93). Knowledge, therefore, is "intimately bound up with power" (Burr, 1995, p. 64) because all versions of events and stories about how the world should be shape social practices and ways of being. They authorise and legitimise some ways while marginalising alternative ways of acting and behaving. Burr (1995) suggests that

> the power to act in particular ways, to claim resources, to control or to be controlled depends upon the 'knowledges' currently prevailing in society. We can exercise power by drawing upon discourses [or knowledges—words added] which allow our actions to be represented in an acceptable light. (p. 64)

Different knowledges establish different hierarchies of practices, people and things. The different knowledges available in any social context are also differentially recognised and thus might have different weightings. Some knowledges become dominant while others are suppressed or completely pushed out of awareness. When a particular knowledge becomes dominant or ascendant, it also disqualifies alternative knowledges, which disadvantages some groups of people while serving the interests of others. White and Epston (1990) claim that subjugated or local knowledges can be "denied or deprived of the space in which they could be adequately performed." They only survive at the margins of society, excluded "from the domain of the formal knowledges and accepted sciences" (p. 26). It is often the expert knowledges of professionals that are valued over, for example, students' experiences of their own lives.

All ways of knowing are exercises of power in some way. However, Foucault (1995, 2000c) distinguished power that is exercised through knowledge from power that uses force or coercion to oppress people. He emphasised that power/knowledge should not be thought of as a commodity that can become someone's individual possession. The power of knowledge actually produces relationships, practices and identities. It is constitutive of social life and culture. It shapes people's actions, because people want to fit the ideals or norms that socially available knowledges prescribe. We will discuss this notion of power in more detail in Chapter 5, where we talk about discourses.

Foucault used the concept of power/knowledge in relation to

disciplines to explain how wider social processes can establish privileged status for some practices and people, along with the marginalisation of others. We suggest, however, that people engage in the process of constructing knowledges as dominant or subjugated, and that they also use knowledges to shape their practices in their personal relationships. When we define and represent things and people in particular ways, we also act upon their actions and we influence and shape what they can or cannot do. This is why Burr (1995) suggests that "[k]nowledge is a power over others, the power to define others" (p. 64). It matters which knowledge, or whose account of an event, becomes dominant and whose account might be denied space or be excluded altogether. The decision to include or exclude certain events in a story can be a technique of power. A person's actions might be deemed morally acceptable in some accounts but unacceptable in others. So it matters how a story is told about a person or an event.

A brief account of a historical event by Czech writer Milan Kundera (Fish, 1999, p. 60) demonstrates how the construction of a particular truth relies on a selective inclusion of some things and the erasure of others. Kundera recalls how communist leader Klement Gottwald was standing on the balcony of a palace in 1948 giving a speech to a big crowd. Gottwald did not have a hat in the freezing cold weather so his comrade, Clementis, took off his fur cap and put it on Gottwald's head. There were hundreds of copies of the photograph of this event circulated, but when Clementis was charged with treason and hanged four years later, he was airbrushed out of the photograph by the propaganda section, leaving Gottwald standing on the balcony on his own. All that remained of him was his cap on Gottwald's head. Although there were thousands of witnesses to this event, the photo taken of it, which was meant to be an exact replica of what the crowd saw, provided an incomplete picture of who was on that balcony. However, those not present at the scene, and members of subsequent generations, might have come to accept the photographic version as the truth, which reinforced only Gottwald as a historically significant person.

Of course, every telling of an event always has gaps, because it is impossible to remember and repeat every detail. This example demonstrates, however, that the deliberate 'selection in' of certain things, and the simultaneous erasure of others, can locate persons differently in a power hierarchy, supporting at the same time a particular story about their character and identity.

We could say that Anna also airbrushed some pertinent details out of the story of her relationship with John, which in turn resulted in positioning John as perpetrator. Her version of the events was privileged by Andrew, while the knowledge John and Marian had about Anna's and John's relationship was disqualified, or, more precisely, it could not be adequately performed and entered into the discussion. Anna's version informed and shaped Andrew's response, along with Andrew's knowledge of unequal power relationships between males and females in society. Drawing on Anna's story, Andrew could only view her actions as acceptable and John's actions as deplorable. John came to be defined as a stalker while Anna was defined as a victim. John could only complain privately to Marian, and he had no or very limited opportunities for requesting a clarifying conversation to question the assumptions that informed Anna's and Andrew's stories. John was distressed because what became considered 'the truth' about him was incongruent with his knowledge of himself as a person.

The stances of 'knowing' and 'not-knowing': information processing versus meaning generation

The process of truth production described above and the privileging of expert knowledges over the local knowledges of clients used to be the dominant mode of professionals' interactions with their clients in the so-called psy-disciplines, such as psychology, psychiatry, psychoanalysis and psychotherapy. Many therapists agreed that an alternative approach was needed, one that was able to reduce the detrimental effects of therapists' exclusive preference for acting from an expert position and consistently excluding or disregarding their clients' local and intimate knowledges of their own lives (Parker, 1999). Therapists working within collaborative and narrative frameworks clearly distinguished between expert approaches, described by Anderson and Goolishian (1992) as "the stance of knowing" and its more respectful alternative, "the stance of not-knowing".

We have included here a comparison of these different modes of interaction as described by therapists because we think their articulation of the differences between these two approaches can be helpful for teachers, too. We do not suggest that teachers' work is the same as therapists', but we claim that teacher–student relationships could benefit from teachers distinguishing and fluently making shifts between an expert and a more 'curious' position. In addition, having an awareness of the effects that different approaches to knowledge can produce on students, along with an awareness of how particular knowledges define teacher–student relationships, can support changes to unhelpful interaction patterns (Kecskemeti, 2013).

Anderson and Goolishian (1992) illustrate what they would term a "stance of knowing" by quoting a client, named Bill, who had this to say about his therapists:

> You [the professionals] are always checking me out ... to see if I knew what you knew, rather than find a way to talk with me. You would ask, 'Is this an ashtray?' to see if I knew or not. (p. 25)

Bill saw his therapists as "information-processing machines", who were only interested in finding out whether or not their client knew what they already knew. A considerable proportion of teachers' work also has to do with checking out whether students know what the teacher knows, and they also ask questions similar to the 'Is this an ashtray?' question. Testing and various forms of assessment require teachers to find out how well their students have acquired the content and skills taught to them. Because teachers, in such instances, are looking for what they already know they are also seeking certain answers. In a test situation, for example, there are only a limited number of correct answers. This type of questioning is about *information processing*. Of course, not all teaching and learning is solely about information processing, but there are times when it is the dominant mode of engaging with the material taught.

A conversation in which the professional takes up a 'not-knowing stance' is deliberately conducted in a way that offers space for interpretation rather than checking what is already known. In such a conversation the professional invites clients to give their interpretations of events or issues—a more respectful alternative, in Anderson and Goolishian's (1992) view. The focus is not on judging whether the client can give *the* correct answer to the therapist's questions, but on whether new meanings are generated. The therapeutic encounter provides a conversational space in which it is possible to create new understandings and "to re-relate the events of our lives in the context of new and different meaning" (p. 28). This mode of engagement is focused on *meaning making* rather than information processing.

Meaning making and arriving at new understandings of concepts, events and issues are also part of learning and subject lessons. We suggest, however, that it should be central to conversations teachers have with their students when they perform pastoral care duties. In such conversations, the topic of discussion is usually students' experiences and life events—similar to what happens in therapeutic conversations—and not subject content. Deans and senior teachers frequently interview students about conflicts that happen inside or outside the classroom. Classroom teachers might also conduct class meetings, where problems that affect a community are discussed. In such instances, the stance of certainty that teachers take up to explain new concepts or demonstrate a skill might not be so useful, because it is less likely to facilitate the sharing of interpretations and personal perspectives on issues. A stance of not knowing that invites students into both "re-relating the events of their lives" (Anderson & Goolishian, 1992, p. 28) and generating new meanings and understandings by revising previous interpretations, can be much more productive.

Andrew assumed that he already had access to 'the truth'. If he had allowed John to re-relate the events of his conflict with Anna he would have been more likely to gain co-operation from him. Taking up an expert position and calling John a liar shut down their conversation and silenced John. Similarly, talking to parents from a stance of knowing and telling them how they could sort out their child who frequently gets into trouble might invite resistance, not only towards a teacher but also towards the whole school. In these instances, an understanding of the stance of not knowing, as it is used by therapists, might better support teachers in achieving a satisfactory relational outcome than would the familiar stance of knowing.

Listening and questioning with genuine curiosity

Andrew felt that his intervention with John and Anna might not have been as successful as he hoped it would be. He was unable to forget the image of John's distressed face when leaving his office and he wondered how John was doing. He thought a lot about how he could have conducted his interviews with the two students differently. In a way he was relieved when Marian requested another appointment for John and Anna.

Andrew carefully considered how to start his second interaction with John differently, and this time he said, "John, regarding the complaint that I received about you, I have had a think about this situation. I am sorry that I have not given you a chance to tell how you think about your conflict with Anna and that I have not listened to your side of the story. But here we are again, so I am interested to find out what you could tell me about what happened."

This invitation offered John an opportunity to provide his version of events. Several unpredictable answers could be inserted into the conversational space opened by Andrew, in contrast to his first interaction with John, when there was only space for one predetermined correct answer. This time Anna also included previously left out details in her telling, and she admitted that her telling on John was a form of revenge for a disagreement.

From the different selection of events admitted into the conversation Andrew was able to revise his previous interpretation of what had happened, and he was able to 'compose' a different story about John's and Anna's relationship, one in which John was not a ruthless perpetrator of stalking. Anna apologised to John and this time both students left Andrew's office satisfied with the outcome.

Andrew commented later that, in a busy school day, the allure of acting from a position of certainty and quickly deciding what the 'truth' might be is considerable, because such responses are less time-intensive. However, he acknowledged that acting from a stance of not-knowing and allowing students to give their interpretations creates less resistance. It should be noted here that Andrew already had some familiarity with the differences between these two stances through the professional development in which he was participating. However, he was able to recognise the problems with his first response only *after* it had happened and not during his conversation with John. This shows how strong the influence of certain modes of interacting (or knowledges) can be and how hard it might be for teachers to switch to alternative ways of engaging with students.

In conclusion, we introduce the concept of *open listening* from education and the concept of *genuine curiosity* from therapy. We think both these concepts draw on similar relationship principles and they help further distinguish between the stances teachers have to operate from. They can also support teachers to develop their capacity to shift flexibly between the stances of knowing and not knowing.

Davies (2011b) has developed the concept of *open listening*, drawing on practices used in Reggio Emilia preschools. She describes open listening as both a philosophy and a practice of listening. It is based on one's capacity "to let go of the status quo" and to create openings for new possibilities by giving up "fixed identities and fixed patterns" and understandings. Open listening suspends judgements, prejudices and preconceived assumptions. It requires us to let go of the kind of listening "that looks for the repetition and affirmation of the already known" (p. 120), as information processing would. Open listening, in contrast,

> might begin with what is known, but it is open to the understandings one has of oneself and others, and the relations between them, creatively evolving into something new. Open listening opens up the possibility of new ways of knowing and new ways of being, both for those who listen and those who are listened to. (p. 120)

If Andrew had been able to apply open listening in his first encounter with John, he could have given up his desire to regulate and control the situation and instead have experienced his pastoral care role as dean in ways that might have been different from the status quo; that is, different from his familiar ways of interacting with students. Instead of fixing Anna and John in familiar gender categories, he would have been open to listening to a story that was different from what he initially assumed, one that generated something new about the two students. When, in the end, he was able to listen differently, the story that emerged contradicted his initial assumptions.

In the terms that Deleuze and Guattari (1987) use, the sheer familiarity of the gender story that Andrew was influenced by made it 'striated'. It became a groove that was easy to fall into. More open listening, on the other hand, allowed Andrew to appreciate that there was more smooth space in the relationship between Anna and John than he had at first allowed. In such smooth space it is possible to create richer conversations in which all involved can learn what they did not enter the conversation already knowing. As a result, the relationship issue could take on an unexpected form—and it could be more creatively resolved.

We suggest that adapting a particular mode of questioning from therapy, one that Anderson and Goolishian (1992) call "abundant, genuine curiosity", can make it easier to engage in open listening and to hear what is not yet known. Genuine curiosity means that the professional "positions himself or herself in such a way as always to be in the state of 'being informed' by the client" (p. 29). So instead of the teacher telling the student what to do, or advising the student how to behave in particular situations, the student could provide as-yet-unknown information to an interested teacher who listens with genuine curiosity. In order to facilitate this change in the direction of the information traffic, all teachers would have to do is to ask questions to which they genuinely do not know the answers.

It is easier to ask such questions about students' experiences, opinions and interpretations of events than about some types of subject content, such as dates of historical events, the correct spelling of a word or a mathematical formula. 'Curious' questions are in the style of Socratic questions that bring forward the as-yet-unknown. These are not meant to be rhetorical or pedagogical questions that would provide their own answer or steer the answer in a particular direction. The contrast here is with the dominant mode of teacher questioning, with its objective of searching for knowledge that is already familiar to the teacher and finding out whether the student also possesses the same knowledge.

We suggest that it is possible and more productive for teachers to position themselves as open listeners in certain situations, like the one in which Andrew was involved. In theory, it should not be that difficult for teachers to ask curious questions to which they do not know the answer. However, a considerable amount of teachers' work is to do with informing others—as they might do when they introduce new material and explain a new concept. In these situations they expect students to listen to them. Teachers also search for already-known answers when they want to be informed about students' knowledge of the material taught. Familiarity with the concepts of power/knowledge, dominant and local knowledges and the differences between acting from a stance of knowing and listening with genuine curiosity could support teachers to interrupt familiar striated patterns of interaction in situations where students' knowledges can lead to smoother, unexpected but more productive relational outcomes.

In this chapter we wanted to draw attention to situations when it would be useful for teachers to give up the stance of knowing and to take up instead a stance of listening that is open to the 'not-yet-said', one that supports the emergence of new stories that teachers might develop together with their students. Andrew was willing to abandon his usual stance of certainty and let go of what he assumed to be the only true account of the conflict between John and Anna. Subsequently, a story of relationship emerged that did not fit the usual, dominant patterns of male–female relationships. John also emerged as a character who did not fit categories of dominant masculinities.

Giving students a chance to respond to and enter into the conversational smooth space about their interpretation of an event can prevent locking them in the category of 'bad student'. In this smooth, rather than striated, space, movement can take place or a line of flight can become possible in both teacher–student and student–student relationships. This shift, in turn, can reduce resistance. Taking up a listening stance and asking questions with genuine curiosity is one way of being open to the 'Other' and to their differences. It is also a way of making differences able to be spoken about and admissible into the conversation rather than hiding them or subsuming them within a familiar dominant story.

Summary of main points in Chapter 3

- A person's knowledge about how the world should be can be validated or rejected, silenced or discarded.
- It is not possible to represent precisely an undistorted image of the world.
- It is easier to persuade teachers to apply the stance of certainty because they are engaged in the transfer of a body of knowledge in the disciplines they teach.
- A postmodern view is that knowledge is a *construction* or a particular version of the world that has been granted the stamp of 'truth'.
- Knowledge is closely tied up with power.

- Some knowledges become dominant, while others are suppressed or pushed out of awareness.
- Knowledge actually produces relationships, practices and identities.
- Social processes establish privileged status for some practices and people, along with the marginalisation of others.
- It matters which knowledge, or whose account of an event, becomes dominant.
- Every telling of an event always has gaps, and certain things are selected and others are erased.
- Teacher–student relationships could benefit from teachers shifting from an expert to a more curious, not-knowing position.
- Open listening involves staying open to current understandings evolving into something new.
- It is not too difficult for teachers to ask curious questions to which they do not know the answer.

Figure 3: Two different approaches to inquiry

What the teacher already knows		What the student knows
Desire to confirm		Desire to learn
Questions that elicit a fit with the teacher's knowledge		Questions that elicit students' interpretations
Certainty		Curiosity
Reproduces the familiar		Generates new meanings

Chapter 4 Externalising conversations: "A hundred baits were not enough to catch one fish"

Introduction
In the previous chapters we have shown the exclusionary effects of categorising young people as problematic and of closing down opportunities to enter into a conversation information that contradicts the status quo. In this chapter we want to reiterate that authoring one's identity is a relational process, and that transcending negative category membership cannot be achieved by students—or by anyone for that matter—alone.

We introduce the notion of externalising and the process of externalising conversations as a method of supporting students not only with becoming different, but also with maintaining a different identity over time, especially in circumstances when to sustain the positive changes achieved by an individual student might require *intensive collective work* from both the student and others involved with her or him. We demonstrate how this collective work can be done and how information gathered in externalising conversations can be put to work to support the re-authoring of the identities of students who are at risk of being stood down, suspended or expelled from school. Rather than policing the boundaries of what counts as normal, externalising can support stretching those boundaries and help students take up an acceptable identity position.

"We all know where he is going to end up"

When Tim arrived at his new school, Mystery Creek High, at the age of 13, his file contained many entries, with details of his recurring problematic behaviour. His new form teacher, Mr Ball, compiled a long list of his past actions that included verbal and physical violence against other children, including swearing, kicking and punching, and verbal abuse of teachers. Mr Ball was aware that Tim had been known to the police from age 7. On occasions he had tried to break into cars and had set fires in deserted buildings. Mr Ball was also aware that Tim used to frequently intimidate other students by stealing their lunches or demanding they hand over their food, threatening violence if they refused to do so. He also continued to do this in Mystery Creek High. When asked by his teachers to do a simple task in the classroom, Tim was likely to respond with swearing, or he would simply storm out of the class and refuse to carry out the teacher's instructions.

Tim's primary school teachers described him as a violent and aggressive child, and in his last year of primary school he was referred to the Severe Behaviour Service for a psychological assessment. The teachers believed Tim showed symptoms of having either conduct or oppositional defiant disorder. A paediatrician diagnosed Tim with ADHD and he was put on a dose of Ritalin. However, according to his own admission, he did not take his medication regularly. Tim was overheard saying to some students and teachers that he had sold some of his Ritalin tablets to make money. He also said that his parents, who were drug addicts, had exchanged the tablets for other drugs. As a result, this medical intervention did not improve Tim's behaviours as much as his primary school teachers expected them to, which upset the principal. However, Tim's teachers received specialist advice from a special education adviser, and Tim was receiving weekly support from an RTLB (Resource Teacher: Learning and Behaviour). In addition, a behaviour support worker supervised him for 2 hours every day and she also taught him anger management strategies.

Over the years the primary school had tried to involve Tim's parents in his education numerous times, but the parents never managed to turn up to pre-arranged meetings. In the absence of collaboration between school and home, the school used a range of punitive measures with Tim on a regular basis. He was kept in during lunch intervals or after school and had to pick up rubbish from the fields and play areas. His computer privileges were curtailed, and he was banned from playing games during intervals for days or for a week at a time. Once he was banned from a class trip, which he took badly and broke some of the chairs in his classroom in retaliation for what he called unjust treatment. He was stood down many times and suspended twice, but the board of trustees gave him another chance and he was allowed to return to his regular class.

None of the interventions seemed to make a difference. Tim continued to refuse to comply with school rules. Instead of showing remorse, he seemed to be proud of the number of punishments he had accumulated. When he received a new punishment, he was heard by teachers saying, "Just add it to the tab", as if mimicking some notorious traffic offenders shown in police programmes on television. He told other students that he was "the man", and that receiving punishments was cool because it showed you were not scared of adults. When Tim's last primary school year came to an end, his class teacher felt relieved, knowing that Tim would move on to Mystery Creek High at the start of the following school year. He said to his colleagues that he was thankful that "that horrible child" had finally moved on. He added, "We all know where he is going to end up. It is not a question of *if* but *when*."

When Tim first came to the attention of the police at the age of 7 the police initially worked closely with his family. The community constable regularly visited the family with a social worker and they tried to support Tim's parents to tighten their supervision of their children and also to establish daily routines. Tim's mother and father managed to make some temporary changes, but things always returned to how they had been previously as both parents struggled with drug addiction. Some days they were so much under the influence of drugs that the children had to take care of them and also of themselves. From the age of 7 Tim had regularly looked after his younger siblings, two brothers and one sister, who were between the ages of 1 and 5 at the time. He would play with them in the street or walk with them to his Nana's house when he felt his parents were totally "out of it". He would feed his youngest brother and sister if there was food at home, or he would steal a chocolate or a packet of biscuits from the dairy if he found the cupboard empty, while his parents were asleep on the couch or away in the pub. As Tim got older and bigger, he became more brazen and started stealing electrical goods from stores, which he then sold.

The police referred Tim's family to the local child protection agency when Tim was 8. They initiated a number of interventions with Tim's parents, but they had not managed to achieve lasting changes to their parenting behaviours. The child protection agency removed the children from the parents' care a few times, placing them with various relatives, such as with their grandparents and an aunt. However, before long, Tim and his siblings ended up running away from their foster parents back to their own parents. They always vehemently defended their parents, as they felt they had been unfairly criticised by relatives and police. Just before Tim was due to start at Mystery Creek High, he and his siblings were placed in foster care with one of their aunties because his parents had started serving a prison sentence for drug dealing and possession. This time the children stayed with their aunt.

Tim's new form teacher, Mr Ball, and his new principal were proponents of a restorative approach to behaviour problems. They frequently used restorative chats and class meetings to discuss problems, and together with the school counsellor and the deans of the school they conducted mediations between students involved in conflict. The majority of teachers at Mystery Creek High believed that such conversations were not just a form of soft discipline that critics would say do not make people accountable. They believed it was much harder for the students to front up and have a face-to-face conversation with an adult and the person they had hurt—about the effects of their wrongdoing on others and about what they could offer to do differently—than picking up rubbish or being held in a room while their peers were playing outside.

Tim was also referred to the school counsellor, who had several conversations with him about the problem of frequently hurting others and getting into trouble as a result. Tim identified anger as a problem that he thought he was struggling with. In subsequent conversations the counsellor invited Tim to tell how anger affected his relationships with different others, including teachers and students, and his learning, and whether it interfered with any of his favourite activities. He was challenged to reflect on ideas that normalised and supported violent ways of responding to others, such as the idea that minimising the seriousness of the punishments he accumulated over time was something to be proud of, as it could earn him the status of 'the man'. He was also asked to evaluate why he wanted his actions to be shaped by such ideas. As the academic year progressed Tim was involved in fewer and fewer conflicts. He was not reported for any offence against the school rules during the last term of the year.

At Mystery Creek High, students like Tim were invited to act as consultants to other students who struggled with similar problems, after a period of proving they could have some influence over the problems that previously had held them in their grip. This involved, among other things, writing a story about how they had managed to reduce the influence of a particular problem, based on conversations students might have had with the counsellor and other supporting adults. These stories were then formatted and published by the students themselves, often with support from a teacher aide, and then shared with other students, or taken home to be read to or by family members. Tim spent a few sessions working on his story with his teacher aide. We will provide excerpts from his story in order to show how writing such stories can be used to support the transcending of a problematic category. The opportunity to write such stories can provide for students the experience of becoming different from before, and can lead to their recognition as 'appropriate' and as recognisable subjects.

What can we make of Tim's story?

When a student regularly misbehaves and transgresses school rules it is easy to see him or her as the problem. Tim's primary school class teacher described him using adjectives—"horrible", "violent" and "aggressive"—that conjured up the image of a bad person who could do nothing right. These adjectives also implied that the problem resided inside Tim, as if he had something wrong with his core. The class teacher only selected for telling Tim's anti-social behaviours, beating up and threatening others, and he formulated an account of him from these actions, as if they made up the totality of him.

There was no space left, in this account, to entertain other possibilities or to include some of his actions that would support another identity description. The part of Tim's life where he performed caring acts towards others, such as looking after both his siblings and his parents and taking on a parenting role at a very young age, were omitted from this account. Yet these acts could also have been interpreted as expressions of responsibility towards others, and they could have formed the basis of an alternative account about him. They would also have proved that the violent actions he committed against classmates were not the totality of who he was. He could have been shown to have not just one but multiple identities.

The omission of these acts, however, ensured that a singular, coherent plot was created about Tim, which was exclusively about violence and aggression. No events were included that would mess up the coherence of this plot. The logic of such a story could not accommodate the tension and contradiction that the inclusion of *both* his harmful actions *and* his capacity to show care and responsibility for others would create.

Tim stepped into the positions that had been offered to him in the story that was circulated about him. He willingly took up what he saw as the 'cool' identity of being 'the man'. There were no other positions available for him within the primary school context besides that of offender and transgressor of rules. The regular dishing out of punishments and his exclusion from activities that rewarded compliant others, such as computer games and class trips, reinforced and reproduced him as someone outside the norm, a person who did not have an acceptable identity. These were, to an extent, coercive interventions that attempted to regulate him by turning him into a "docile body" (Foucault, 1995) while demonstrating the power of the school to everyone. He did not receive recognition for acting appropriately.

Sending him for a psychological assessment further reinforced the internal origins of his problems. There was something wrong inside Tim, which could be brought to awareness with an assessment and then responded to with some kind of treatment. This approach is based on a medical model, which likens humans to machines. In the terms that Deleuze and Guattari (1977) outline, it is a 'machinic' model of treating him. It assumes that persons are made up of parts, which, when broken, are possible to repair with the right treatment, just as it is possible to weld a broken pipe. Of course, not all psychologists and psychiatrists work from these assumptions. However, Tim's paediatrician did and Tim was given medication, which was meant to produce chemical changes in his body, which in turn would calm him down so that he did not respond with violence. The social and relational production of violence, through its glorification in computer games, films, television programmes and its availability as a possible identity model for young boys, was not taken into consideration in this approach. Neither was there an acknowledgment that some of Tim's law breaking, such as stealing food from the dairy and selling stolen goods for money, was to support the basic survival needs of his siblings and himself.

We do not condone Tim's behaviours and neither do we suggest that anything goes when survival is at stake. However, Tim's actions raise the question of how we are to conceptualise responsibility. Is Tim solely and individually responsible for all his anti-social behaviours, or is a notion of shared responsibility more helpful to make sense of his actions? Can he be made responsible for his parents' actions when he and his siblings are hungry? What collective responsibility do child protection agencies, the police or communities have, if any, to ensure that children like Tim, who might have irresponsible parents incapable of looking after their children for various reasons, don't go to bed hungry? How can we tell the difference between an unlawful act that is purposely committed to harm others, and an unlawful act, such as stealing food and other things for money, that is committed to meet basic needs? Is it possible to consider an individual person's actions as completely separate from other individuals, or are individuals entangled and intra-acting with each other and their circumstances and material environments in complex ways, as Barad (2007) suggests? These questions, we think, will prompt very different answers from those who believe it is possible to live life as an autonomous individual, independent of others, than from those who believe no one can exist independently of others and their material circumstances. The theoretical ideas introduced in this chapter help reflect on these issues more fully.

Analysis of Tim's story

Storying lives and relationships: The trap of singular identity narratives

We have previously talked about how people interpret and make meanings of events when they perform their identities. We have also talked about the far-reaching effects of single names, labels and categorisations on people's practices and identities. In this chapter we are concerned with how single names and categories can be used as themes around which a series of events can be woven together to create self-narratives and narratives about others. White and Epston (1990) suggest that people create such narratives by "arranging their experiences of events in sequences across time in such a way as to arrive at a coherent account of themselves and of the world around them" (p. 10). As no particular narrative can include every single experience that a person has had, people have to select and link events together in a sequence that fits a particular plot of their and of others' relationships, abilities, actions and hopes. Thus, most experiences of an individual will never be told, or they will be left out of some of the stories they and others tell about themselves and the world.

As every single narrative is a product of selection and omission, which makes it possible to create a plot, no single narrative can adequately represent or describe a person's identity or a person's lived experiences. There will always be "significant and vital aspects" (White & Epston, 1990, p. 40) of people's experiences and lives that will be left out, even from the dominant narratives they tell about themselves because they contradict the plot of that narrative. The dominant narrative that was created about Tim in his primary school included only his aggressive responses towards other children and some of his unlawful activities outside school. These events fitted the 'horrible child' plot and also told a story of Tim possibly ending up in prison. The structure of the story could not accommodate other events that contradicted it, such as Tim's care for his siblings and parents.

Change can be extremely problematic when a singular story about a person becomes dominant and when it is treated as the one and only true account of that person. We can call it a totalising account (Winslade & Monk, 2007). Singular, totalising stories silence other accounts and blind people to the possibility of storying lives and experiences as multiple and contradictory. Tim could be storied not only as an aggressor but also as a caring person who loves his siblings and is loyal to his parents. He could also be storied as a student who wants *both* to comply with school rules, because he wants to please his parents, *and* to refuse to follow the rules, because he finds being 'the man' attractive. However, a singular plot narrative, of either violence or caring, cannot accommodate Tim's shifts between his changing and contradictory desires and actions, because they would destroy the coherence of the plot.

Lagermann (2014) suggests that such singular plot stories are based on binary thinking, which can only consider students as *either/or*, good or bad, categorising them as either troublemakers and aggressors, or as compliant and co-operative. These singular categories can become 'sticky' and very hard for students to shake off, because they form the basis of the narratives that are circulated about them as the only true representations of who they are. Such singular identity narratives fix and trap students in particular identities, closing down opportunities to transcend negative categories and to experience themselves as becoming a recognised subject. "Binary thinking makes us blind to the numerous intermediate in-betweens, to multiplicity and to processes of differenciation (sic)" (p. 15).

Becoming recognised only as an undesirable person starts to take on the features of what Nelson (2001) calls a "mandated identity". It can also block students from becoming other than what they were before. It is worth noting in this regard that, in its etymological origins, the word 'identity' means 'staying the same'. The problem is that once it is assigned, an identity becomes difficult to shift, even though it is also true that people are changing all the time. Tim was trapped in the 'horrible child' identity without being given any opportunities to expand that position and to experience himself being recognised as a caring person.

Instead of accepting a single story as the true and total account of a person, we should look for events in a person's life that might have previously been neglected, unnoticed and consequently left out of the stories that they and others tell about them as representations of who they are. We suggest that it is easier to notice such events if we deliberately locate problems outside people.

In the end the choice is an ethical one. We can choose to see people like Tim through the lens of a singular story that condemns him from the start as a bad person and that continually reproduces negative judgements of him as essentially guilty of being a bad person and seeks to control his behaviour. If we make this choice we can expect to have to keep on working against him and minimising the elements of his life that affirm more positive tendencies. We would have to do things that manage his problematic behaviour by crimping his whole existence. Or we can look at his life from a different angle altogether, as a complex and rich array of storylines. We can start from the assumption that he is capable of "becoming somebody" (Smyth & Hattam, 2004) on his own terms, given the chance. We can work to understand the lines of force that constitute his life and appreciate the ways in which he uses these, sometimes creatively, even if there are other times when his responses are more muddled. We can start from the assumption that he is not a bad person needing to be judged harshly, but a person whose life does not easily fit into narrow categories, such as good or bad. Rather than seeking to crimp his existence, we can see him through the lens of curiosity as someone trying his best to create a life and someone who might understandably sometimes react to how he is treated by others.

Externalising: Separating problems from persons and opening up movement

Problems can be conceived of as originating in persons, an internalising approach, or as originating outside persons, which White (1988, 2007) terms 'externalising'. Deleuze (1993) argues that we fold events into ourselves from the outside to form identities anyway. The externalising approach separates persons from problems, claiming 'The problem is the problem, the person is never the problem'. Tim's previous class teacher only noticed what he had considered deficient about Tim. He identified him as the problem, and, by his use of the adjectives "horrible", "violent" and "aggressive", he attributed the origin of the problem of violence to something that resided inside Tim. These adjectives became labels that placed Tim in the category of aggressive and violent persons. As identities, they served as convenient explanations for subsequent actions that might have fitted the same category.

The allocation of such category membership to him excluded the possibility of the class teacher noticing when he might have behaved according to the rules. His inappropriate actions were seen as manifestations of his inner "core" (Morgan, 2000), so he was only recognised by the school as problematic, which made it impossible for him to gain validation as a responsible person. The narrative that was circulated about Tim only included events from his life that supported a negative identity description (White & Epston, 1990). This story shaped how his class teacher, and possibly some other teachers and some students, saw Tim. In other words, this story constituted Tim as an undesirable subject. Moreover, in some way Tim sensed what was going on and nurtured a sense of injustice, which fuelled his responses that locked him (in others' eyes) further into the category of an undesirable person.

Externalising, or the externalisation of problems, offers a different orientation in response to the behaviour problems Tim performed. Externalising is both a conversational move and a particular epistemological position that is based on a belief that problems are relationally and socially produced, as opposed to being owned by or residing within individuals. Externalising starts with a shift in language use that "encourages persons to objectify and, at times, to personify the problems that they experience as oppressive. In this process, the problem becomes a separate entity and thus external to the person or relationship that was ascribed as the problem" (White & Epston, 1990, p. 38).

In Tim's case, instead of describing him with adjectives such as violent and aggressive, which internalise his actions, through a linguistic shift of turning adjectives into nouns his actions could be nominalised as a violence or aggression that is influencing him. Violence is a line of force that he hitches himself to rather than something that originates in him and emerges from him. A space could thus be created between him and his harmful actions. This space would also be more of a smooth rather than a striated space (Deleuze & Guattari, 1987), because it would allow movement through the exploration of the wider landscape that Tim traverses while he shifts between caring and being loyal to his parents and punching others and stealing.

White and Epston (1990) caution that when externalising is used simply as a technique it might achieve something different from what was intended. If externalising remains a simple linguistic manoeuvre and is surrounded by other conversations in which a person's responses are assumed to be representative of the essence of the person, these assumptions will prove more powerful than the grammatical shift. Externalising conversations are meant to be used in ways that interrupt familiar and usual experiences and "create a context where the person experiences themselves as separate from the problem" (Morgan, 2000, p. 24). They are meant to open a space that helps to explore a person's relationship with a problem in a way that offers a new perspective on the problem, one that then helps the person to take different actions or to overcome their sense of failure or inadequacy. As White and Epston (1990) explain, "… These practices do not separate persons from responsibility for the extent to which they participate in the survival of the problem" (p. 65). They do, however, help to make visible the extent to which such responsibility is shared with relational and cultural forces.

Had Tim's former teachers been able to see aggression and violence as separate from Tim, as a line of force influencing him rather than as a representation of the essential Tim, they might also have been able to look for and notice events from Tim's life that supported a different identity description. Subsequently, Tim might have been able to use his caring for his siblings to reduce the appeal of being 'the man', for example. Other ways of becoming a man that Tim might have had available to him could have been explored too. We will explain in more detail how externalising conversations can provide opportunities for students to experience themselves as multi-storied and changing—in the process of becoming (Davies, 2009), as opposed to being frozen in a single category—when we introduce excerpts from a story written by Tim about 'Anger'.

Change as ongoing, collective work

Shifting the location of the problem from inside to outside persons makes visible a number of things about how problem narratives and problematic identities are produced, but also about how they could be changed. We want to highlight two important aspects of achieving change, both of which, we believe, remain hidden when problems are located in individuals. First, for a student or anyone to see their way out of a negative identity category, they need someone who relates to them in a different way from how they are usually recognised. Second, even when there is someone who provides such different recognition and acknowledges the person as an appropriate subject, the change achieved in a person's understanding of themselves "must be worked on continuously/iteratively" (Lagermann, 2014, p. 10). We will set Tim's story aside for a moment and introduce Amir from Lagermann's (2014) research in order to indicate that people cannot move beyond or shake off marginal or negative identity positions on their own. Amir's example also shows that becoming someone else, more than just temporarily, requires ongoing collective work, because the intensity of the effects of events and actions that support changes can be lost over time.

Amir is a 9th-grade Danish student who sees himself as a troublemaker. However, when he is sent to a technical college as part of a transition programme, his teacher, Glenn, responds to him differently from most of his regular college teachers. Glenn uses humour and gets involved in the activities the students have to do, such as building a tree house, and, with his help, Amir is able to finish set tasks. He achieves credits for his work. According to Amir, Glenn knows "how to handle us troublemakers" (p. 13). Glenn is recognisable to Amir because he acts in ways Amir's friends do. He uses humour and banter in the same way, so the atmosphere he creates is familiar to Amir. In this familiar climate Amir is able to complete challenging learning tasks and he is able to expand his previous identity category of troublemaker. He becomes someone different, a good student, and he is recognised by Glenn as such.

Thus Glenn is influential in the kind of student subject Amir can become, as he is able and willing to provide experiences for him that are different from the ones he had with previous teachers. Amir becomes a meaningful subject both to himself and to his teacher. However, these experiences make it more difficult for him to go back to his regular school, where he is still seen by most teachers as the troublemaker. He applies to transfer to Glenn's class but the school does not respond to his application, so he is unable to shake off the troublemaker label. When the researcher meets him 3 years later he has finished 10th grade in another school and has dropped out of technical college after the first half year. Although he had seen himself in new ways when he was in Glenn's class, as different from a troublemaker, he has not been able to maintain this different identity over time. No other teacher has provided repetitive citations and iterations of Amir as the good student like Glenn did. Yet, in order for Amir to be able to maintain his new identity, and to stay out of the category of troublemaker, the kind of continuous iterative work that Glenn did is vital. Amir needs others—not just himself—to affirm and validate him in the position of good student.

In his primary school there was similarly no one who would relate to Tim differently from how he was repeatedly and routinely recognised there. Fortunately for him, Mr Ball and his colleagues at Mystery Creek High were able to view him as separate from the problem of aggression and they were willing to look for actions and events in his life that would support a validation of him as someone other than just a violent and aggressive person. The teachers at Mystery Creek High also found ways to collectively provide the repetitive affirmations of Tim as separate from problems, which supported him to transcend a negative identity category through re-authoring a problem narrative into an alternative one.

Alternative identities: Creating and maintaining movement

Re-authoring a person's relationship with the problem

We mentioned before that at Mystery Creek High the teachers responsible for the pastoral care of students often had externalising conversations with them. At the end of this chapter we have included some helpful questions that can be adapted to discuss a variety of problems as separate from persons. We hope that teachers will find them useful in opening up the space to entertain other possibilities about those students who teachers and other students have only been able to cite as having a problematic identity—that is, as identical with problems, as opposed to separating them from problems. Rather than dwelling on the technicalities of externalising conversations, we want to show the kinds of previously invisible things about a person that can become available for exploration, when the location of the problem is shifted from inside a person to outside, into the social and relational arena. The following excerpt is from such an alternative story that Tim was supported to both create and circulate about himself. He chose to give it the title "A hundred baits were not enough to catch one fish".

A hundred baits were not enough to catch one fish

I used to fight dirty and I used to punch and kick people. I even broke into cars. I let my life to be ruled by Anger and I let it convince me that it was OK to do all these things that got me into serious trouble. When I came to this school, I was first mean to the other kids. I threatened them and made them give me their lunches. I used to be angry with them, when they stared at me. But a few weeks after I moved in with my aunty and when my parents went to prison, I decided to stop Anger. I just said to myself, "That's enough. I don't want Anger to win any more."

It has been 8 months now that I have managed to keep Anger away. I probably couldn't have done it without the help of my teachers and the principal in my new school. My foster aunty helped me the most. She taught me to finish my work, she sat down with me to do my homework, she gave me a lot of her own time, and she talked to me—and all that helped me a lot to keep Anger away.

I don't want my classmates to see me as an angry and violent person. I want them to know that I can also be a good friend. I care about people, like I have always cared about my brothers and sister. I know I can look after people, because I used to look after my parents when they struggled with drugs. My parents want me to be a kind person and they want me to finish school. My Nana and my aunty, the one I am staying with at the moment, also want me to stay out of trouble. I don't want other kids to be scared of me. I don't want to be like one of my uncles who beats up his kids.

Mr Ball, my teacher, helped me most by talking to me and by telling me the "Story of the Fish". The fish was swimming in the sea and there were hundreds of baits around him, but he could avoid them all, because he made sure he would not bite on any of them. Mr Ball told me that I could pretend to be this fish and imagine that the students who were teasing me were the baits. If I answered their teasing by fighting back, it meant that I bit on their bait, and I was caught in trouble. I practised to avoid the hundred baits (the teasing, calling me names) that were

> around me every day, trying to catch me. But they could not catch me!
>
> The baits are still there, and always will be, but I have learnt how to deal with them. I think I am strong enough to keep Anger away on my own now, but if Anger got a bit stronger, I have got people who, I am sure, would be happy to help me.

Re-authoring relationships with others

Mr Ball did not just talk about the problem with Tim. He also conducted a class meeting in response to some students' concerns about Tim. When Tim arrived at his new school, during the first few days he used his height to intimidate his peers, ordering them to surrender their lunches or money to him. Several of the students felt threatened, and believed that if they did not comply with his wishes they would suffer serious consequences. They complained to the principal and to Mr Ball.

Mr Ball took the complaints seriously and organised a class meeting. Tim's classmates collectively decided that he should not be at the meeting as his presence would silence the other students. They would inform him of the outcomes later. There was considerable distress in the class meeting that followed when, one by one, Tim's classmates recounted how he had acted violently towards others. Acknowledging the seriousness of the situation and validating their concerns, Mr Ball summarised what they had told using externalising language:

> It sounds like Tim lets himself be guided and advised by serious bullying tactics and violence that cause much harm to others. The violence used by him makes most of you feel unsafe in the class and often outside the class as well and there are times when some of you don't even want to come to school. You don't want to sit close to him, because you can't tell if you have to put up with threats of violence.

The class spent considerable time discussing the effects of Tim's actions. Everyone agreed that the harassment and violence had to stop. Continuing to use externalising, Mr Ball asked, "Are there times when Tim manages to free himself from the influence of violence?" His classmates readily provided examples of Tim's kindness and collaboration.

The students also discussed how they wanted him to be accountable to them on a daily basis. Their teacher asked, "How could Tim prove to you that he is changing his relationship to violence?" The students suggested several small changes to how the class enters and leaves rooms when lessons start or finish, suggesting Tim be the last to enter or leave, as that would minimise his opportunities for banging the door on others. A plan was drawn up and presented to Tim, and follow-up was carried out by one of the deputy principals Tim had to report to daily. Tim stayed out of trouble for the rest of the school year.

Class meetings like the one Mr Ball facilitated have to be carefully conducted. They can easily be turned into a humiliating exercise if they are simply used to give advice to the wrongdoer or to dish out collectively thought-out punishments (Leach & Lewis, 2013). They can also be focused so much on supporting the wrongdoer to create an alternative identity description that they can be experienced by victims of bullying as letting the wrongdoer off the hook without making him or her accountable.

Externalising conversations did not change the unhelpful cultural ideas that support violence in relationships and that had been extensively available to Tim to fold into his identity. However, they changed, even if temporarily, his positioning in relation to those ideas. It became possible for him to take responsibility for his wrongdoing and to ponder the effects of his aggressive behaviour, not only on others, but also on his own future possibilities and potential life trajectories. He was able to consider the identity positions he wanted to take up and the positions he wanted to reject, which, in turn, helped him articulate his preferred identity. He could see beyond the category of violent and horrible persons and he was able to imagine himself as a caring person who can look after others. The opportunities he had for re-authoring his relationship to violence also led to altering the ways he conducted his relationships with his classmates.

Documenting alternative identity stories and positioning students as consultants

As we mentioned before, it was customary at Mystery Creek High to publish stories like the one Tim put together, based on his conversations about anger with his school counsellor and Mr Ball. Recording in writing his changed relationship with anger provided opportunities for him to repeatedly experience himself as different from being violent and aggressive. As a consultant to other students who also struggled with anger, he was asked to share his story with his peers a number of times. Tim also took his story home and read it to his foster auntie and Nana. The writing and sharing of the story provided those continuous and repetitive iterations of him as an appropriate subject that we described previously as vital for any identity changes to be maintained. An audience was recruited for Tim, who collectively acknowledged him as different from before, helping him to experience and understand himself as other than a member of the category of violent persons, and more of an authority on his own life (Epston & White, 1992).

Schools, workplaces, hospitals and other institutions document various pieces of information about persons that are stored in files or other professional documents. Such information is often used to define and construct persons in particular ways. White and Epston (1990) claim that, most often, the subject of professional documents is a person who is being evaluated, while the author of the document about them is someone "skilled in the rhetoric pertaining to a specific domain of expert knowledge" (p. 188). When experts appropriate and transfer a person's experiences into the domain of their expert knowledge, the document they produce can support exclusionary practices, through evaluating a person against normalising judgements (Winslade, 2013).

Alternative documents, such as the kind of self-narrative that Tim produced, achieve different effects. First, they are "authored by the person who is their subject" (White & Epston, 1990, p. 191). The author, therefore, "plays a central role in contributing to the specification of her own self" (p. 191). Secondly, they can be shared with a much wider readership or audience, in contrast to files, which are usually kept locked in a filing cabinet or stored on a computer and are shared only among professionals. By making his story available to his immediate community, Tim was able to constitute himself and his life in ways that contradicted and interrupted the negative repetitive citations about him. He was able to call on support from others when producing himself as someone who was finding a path out of the category of violence.

Anger as the product of intra-action

Davies (2014b) proposes, based on her observations of children in a kindergarten setting, that rage or anger do not belong exclusively to certain individuals. They are the products of *intra-actions* between individuals, where one person affects and is being affected by the other, during the process of each individual working to ensure his or her own continued inclusion in their social group. Tim wanted to belong, but when people stared at him or teased him, he experienced it as exclusion and responded with anger that was not always unreasonable. His desperate move to steal food from the dairy was brought on both by his concern for his siblings and by his parents' inability to provide responsible care for their children. At Mystery Creek High the teachers' actions were based on the belief that everyone was implicated in, and therefore had responsibility for, producing either viable or non-viable lives (Butler, 2004b). This meant that Tim's actions were viewed not as his sole responsibility but as the product of many others affecting him and being affected by him. Therefore, the support organised around him was provided by several people who worked together to perform the kind of ongoing collective work that could overwrite or erase the repetitive citations of him as a violent person.

Stretching the boundaries of normal

Discussing common relationship patterns with young children

Even in primary schools, children could be asked to write about common relationship problems—such as anger, bullying, teasing, arguments, spreading rumours about others—in the manner Tim did. It is possible to name these problems and then discuss their effects, with children recounting a personal experience with a particular problem and describing its effects on their significant relationships, activities and hopes. It is also possible to ask them what they think supports the maintenance of such problems, touching on social processes that reproduce particular ways of being as dominant, normal and acceptable, while suppressing alternative ways of behaving.

Quite young children are aware of how the media, video and computer games, and books and relational practices used by some people might legitimise and promote as desirable ways of behaving that are harmful to others. They might also be aware of the dominance of certain patterns of behaviour in their immediate communities and they have some understanding of how alternative ways might be discouraged or suppressed completely. Young children draw on these social 'models', just like adults do. It is possible to make children more aware of the social production of relationship practices and to go beyond seeing them as simply the character fault of particular individuals. In Chapters 5 and 6 we will discuss in more detail how it is possible to invite children to think about how particular practices might advantage some people while oppressing others.

Summary of main points in Chapter 4

- This chapter introduces the practice and the logic of externalising.
- Externalising contrasts with internalising accounts of a person's identity, which are often singular accounts that omit contradictory aspects of identity.
- Singular accounts fit people into identity categories, which frequently totalise them as undesirable persons.
- Externalising is a linguistic shift that turns actions into nouns and is also an epistemological position in which we view people as complex beings.
- Rather than seeing people as frozen in a single identity, externalising allows them to be understood as always becoming.
- For changes to stick, they need to be persisted with through a series of iterations.
- It is possible to externalise feelings, relationship practices, cultural practices, or events.
- You can ask about a problem's tricks and intentions. For example, "How did aggression trick you into doing its wishes again?" or, "What kind of life do tantrums intend for you to lead?"
- After developing an externalisation, it is useful to explore the problem's influence over the person and the person's influence over the problem.
- Teachers can do one-off externalising conversations without doing therapy.

Figure 4: Internalising and externalising

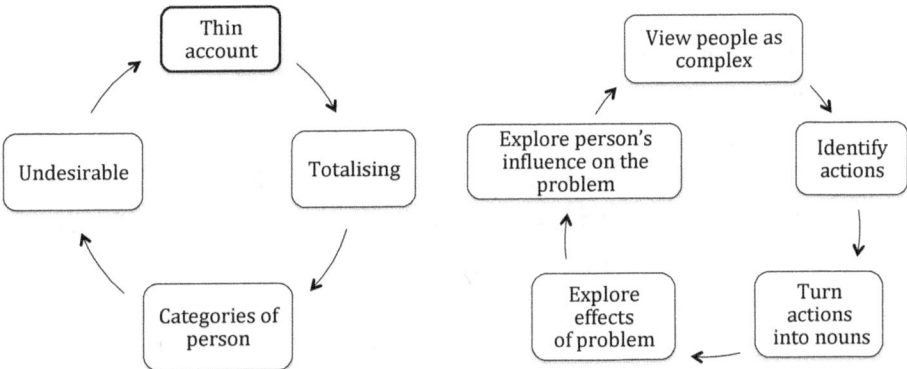

Exercise: externalising and internalising

In pairs, discuss the following statements and mark the ones that you think are externalising statements. Come up with an externalising version for the statements that you think are internalising.

- He is big!!! trouble in the classroom.
- John is often so naughty.
- He lets anger control his life.
- I don't allow fear to ruin the fun that I can have with my friends.
- I blame myself for my son's troubles.
- Guilt is something that many women in our family have struggled with.
- I am really concerned about his anger.
- It's my ADHD that does it, not me.
- I am bad and I am dumb.
- She has put the worries in the box.
- Those children are bullies.
- Let's try to keep trouble out of the classroom together.

In not more than one paragraph, describe a student you teach using externalising language. Choose someone who you think struggles with one or several problems. Try to name the problem and give details about the student's relationship with this problem. Describe the effects the problem has on the student's relationships with significant others and on his or her activities. Describe what influence you think the student might have on the problem.

Externalising conversations: some helpful questions

We have included here a basic four-part structure of an externalising conversation and examples of the types of questions that teachers could ask within each part of an externalising interview with a student who struggles with a problem, similarly to Tim. The questions might need to be modified to suit a particular problem. It is not necessary to ask each question listed here. We have provided a selection so that interested teachers can use them as examples and formulate their own questions. It is possible to compile a selection of questions about an issue that could be used with a whole class to structure discussions or to write about a problem that is affecting class members, in the manner Tim wrote about anger.

1. Naming and describing the problem

- How would you describe the problem that your teachers/parents/friends say you are struggling with? What name would you give to it?
- I was wondering what you would call this problem? Would you call it worry, or self-doubt, or something else?

First, you might have to tell the person what others think the problem might be. However, it is always important to get the description of the person concerned and to ask whether they agree with how others describe the problem. Use the name the person gives to the problem and not the name others have used to describe it.

- How would I know the problem was affecting you? What would I see you doing and saying?

It is possible to externalise:

a. feelings: fear, anger, guilt, jealousy, sadness

b. relationship practices: arguments, fights, bickering, blaming, conflict, co-operation, sharing (or an unwillingness to share), harassment, bullying, temper tantrums, rage, violence

c. cultural practices: mother-blaming, parent-blaming, racism, sexism, homophobia, exclusion, discrimination.

To get more information about the problem, you can ask about its tricks, tactics, plans, allies, and things that fuel it:

- How does worry stop you from trying?
- How does embarrassment convince you that you cannot do it? What is it telling you about yourself? Does it work quickly or slowly?

You can also locate a problem in time and with a history:

- When did the problem appear in your life? What was it like before it?
- How long has the problem managed to wreck your relationships?
- When was the problem the strongest or weakest?

2. The problem's effects

These questions help explore the problem's effects on a person's:

a. sense of self and view of themselves as sister, mother, friend, student, etc.

b. relationships with teachers, friends, family members, others in the community

c. hopes, dreams

d. work, study, hobbies,

e. social life and everyday life (routines)

f. thoughts, feelings, moods

g. health,

 - How has talking affected your relationship with your teachers?
 - How do you think tantrums affected how the other students see you? What kind of person do they think you might be?
 - What effect does anger have on how you view yourself as a son, brother or friend?
 - What are arguments stopping you from doing?
 - What are arguments stopping others from seeing about you?

Evaluating the problem and saying why it should change
- Is it a good or a bad thing?
- Do you like things to be the way they are?
- Is it something you prefer or you would like it to be different?

Invite the person to justify their evaluation. Why? Why not?

3. The person's influence over the problem

These questions help explore what a person can do to reduce the problem's influence. Listen for actions, thoughts, feelings, hopes, dreams, commitments and personal qualities that might reduce the influence of the problem.

- Are there times when the problem is not as bad or is weaker?
- How have you managed to stop the problem from getting worse?
- Can you think of a time when the problem could have prevented you from having a good time, or paying attention, or being kind to your friend, but it didn't? What did you do to achieve that?
- Tell me about a time when you resisted the problem and did what you wanted, instead of letting the problem take control of your life.

Try to get as many details as possible in response to the above question: what happened before and after, how did you prepare yourself, how long did it last, what did your friends say?

Evaluate the unique outcome:

- What does it say about you as a person that you could do this?
- What did it take to be able to resist the problem?
- Who else would be pleased to hear that you could be in charge of your actions instead of letting the problem be in charge?

4. Future plans

- What are you going to do to keep things going?
- What support do you need?

It is possible to have a one-off conversation about problems without doing therapy. The same interview structure can be helpful to talk about issues or problems affecting children, parents and colleagues. However, if students name or imply a problem that is completely beyond their scope of influence—such as stress or difficulties concentrating that might be due to changed adult relationships, violence or abuse at home, or ongoing bullying in the playground—then the problem should be addressed with adults and others in the school community. You might have to involve a student's parents, other professionals such as school counsellors, RTLBs or child protection agencies, a group of students or the whole class.

Question for reflection

Think about times when a student might have 'pushed your buttons'. Try to remember your emotional responses, as well as the ways you spoke about this student to colleagues. What difference might it make if you describe this student using externalising language?

Chapter 5 Problematising discourses of teaching and learning: "I switch off because it is boring. It is your job to teach us anyway"

Introduction

So far we have introduced relationship principles and conversational moves that, we believe, can successfully reduce the effects of normalisation and exclusion. We have shown how these same moves can also support a person's validation and recognition within accepted categories. The relationship practices described in the remaining chapters demonstrate practical applications of the second key assumption this book is based on: it is possible to effectively challenge ideas circulating in the social context that exclude, oppress and disadvantage persons and place teachers and students in conflict with each other.

Each remaining chapter, except for the last, is devoted to introducing a particular process of problematisation and critique. We think each of these processes can help teachers and students understand how ideas or discourses can work as lines of force, and how they can (re-)produce unhelpful or harmful practices and identities if they are not reflected on. We will show that the new understandings arrived at through problematisation can offer more helpful alternatives.

The notion of discourse is a central concept, without which the particular processes of problematisation that we propose cannot be performed. A discursive approach helps locate problems outside persons and can illuminate the relational production of conflict. The examples we provide demonstrate how the pedagogies and relationship practices that teachers employ—and students' various responses to these pedagogies—are all shaped by hidden rationalities or discourses about schooling, relationships, and the role of teachers and students.

Teachers and students draw on a wide range of socially available discourses. Practices and behaviours based on assumptions about schooling and relationships that are dominant in a particular place at a particular time can usually be performed in a habitual manner, without much effort and thought. They can, therefore, become taken for granted and accepted as truths, which can make their harmful effects unavailable for reflection or any kind of scrutiny. Every time such a taken-for-granted practice is performed unexamined and unchallenged, it continues to disadvantage some students or teachers. It is, therefore, important for teachers and students to be familiar with specific processes of problematisation that can trouble the very ideas they might accept as useful but that place them in conflict with each other in ways that are hard to immediately recognise.

A further aim of this chapter is to show that changes in teacher practice resulting from a problem-solving, or 'what works', approach to reflection might not be enough to intervene in 'the lives' of recurring problems in the long run. Relationship problems survive because they are reproduced and maintained by ideas and beliefs—or discourses—about schooling that are available in the social context and that are supported by the organisational practices of schools. Sensitivity to discourses of schooling and an understanding of how those discourses might shape teacher and student practices and identities can prevent the reproduction of relationship problems by offering a different, more productive response to teacher–student conflicts compared to frequent and reactive teacher practice change. Although reflecting on discourses and problematising their effects might not bring the same change that a behaviour management strategy would, the different perspectives it throws up can interrupt or prevent the reproduction of ideas that support destructive emotional responses and relationship practices of disrespect.

We recommend that teachers try the process among themselves first by engaging in collegial conversations to identify the very practices that do not produce the relational outcomes and classroom environments that are conducive to teaching and learning. If teachers are well practised in identifying discourses and understanding some of their long-term effects, it is easier to conduct the class meeting to be introduced in Chapter 6, and to invite students to examine the effects of different discourses of schooling.

Engineering the English programme

Jacob and Leanne, who both teach a class of Year 7/8 students, have shared with their colleagues how stressful they have found students' resistance during their English lessons. Such resistance was mostly produced in response to writing tasks assigned to students. The majority of students refused to complete, or even start, writing when these teachers insisted they do so. Students responded with statements such as, "Why do we have to do this? It is so boring," or they swore and refused to follow instructions. On other occasions teacher requests for task completion escalated into more serious conflict, with some students storming out of class.

Jacob and Leanne compiled a collection of recurring responses students gave when they resisted a challenging task in other subjects. They shared these during departmental discussions and we have included some of them below.

- When the lesson is not fun, I switch off and start talking to others because it is boring.
- Teachers talk too much and it's boring.
- Teachers need to use our language.
- I hate theory, reading texts and doing bookwork because it is hard.
- I do not like sitting and working quietly. Why can't we have more action in every lesson?
- Why do we have to do it over and over again?

- If I like the teacher and the teacher provides interesting activities, then I will do the work.
- It is the teachers' job to teach us and, if I don't understand something, it is their fault.

Writing a story and writing about experiences from memory during English lessons proved to be a particular challenge to many of the students in Jacob's and Leanne's classrooms. Students often used delaying tactics, taking 20 or more minutes to even start writing. This situation troubled Jacob and Leanne greatly because they wanted their students to become good at writing and wanted them to enjoy the activities. They discussed the situation several times, and after much reflection concluded that students would learn better, and would most likely display less resistance to challenging tasks, if they were assigned more interesting and exciting activities. In these two teachers' interpretation this meant the inclusion of more action in their English lessons.

They also agreed that it was theory and the academic aspects of the subject of English that proved difficult for students. As a result they decided to replace activities that involved reading texts, bookwork and sitting quietly with activities they saw as more 'action-packed' and thus more appealing. In practice, this meant that Jacob and Leanne modified almost every English lesson by including at least one activity that involved movement, according to students' preferences. This was how they explained to colleagues the teaching strategies they had started to use on a regular basis to deliver their writing lessons.

Jacob

I've tried to engineer my whole English programme to incorporate things that would draw positive experiences. We do sport and recreation as part of their English group, so we go and play a sport and do something and we come back and write about it and do the literacy part of it. I thought it was pointless for me to sit down, because, you know, sitting down with those boys and giving them texts and read this and try and analyse it, just doesn't work. They dismiss it as boring.

Leanne
In my English lesson, I'm trying to provide experiences, so that, when they come back, they'll want to write. We did this 'Fear Factor' type of stuff in class the other day and I made up all this goo and blindfolded them. Next week, I'm going to take them out and do bubbles. They get a bit high in the first 5 minutes, when we get back into the room, but then they all have got something to write about, because they want to write about something straight after it's happened, not a week later. I just find that kids are much more tactile these days, I mean they expect it. If you want good stuff out of them, you've got to do good stuff with them first.

The students responded positively to these adaptations, with even the most reluctant students willing to write a few sentences about the experiences these two teachers provided in the first half of their writing lessons.

What can we make of Jacob's and Leanne's responses to students' off-task behaviours?

Teachers routinely make daily choices about what pedagogies might best improve their students' engagement with a particular lesson or activity. Irrespective of the subject, the pedagogy chosen in the moment, especially when selected as a response to recurring disruptions and defiance, can either increase or reduce productive lesson time spent on developing students' competencies. When disruptions occur, a 'problem solving' or 'what works' approach might be intuitively more appealing to teachers when deciding what strategy to use. Quickly re-establishing classroom order to allow the lesson to proceed without much time lost on off-task behaviours might become the main short-term priority.

In such cases the immediate effectiveness of a chosen practice as a behaviour management strategy might become the criterion against which the strategy is evaluated, rather than its long-term implications and effects on students. This kind of problem-solving approach has been criticised by proponents of critical pedagogy (Giroux, 2004; St Pierre, 2002), who comment on the instrumental nature of this approach, because it can serve as a barrier to teachers paying closer attention to the wider social and learning implications of different teaching practices.

Leanne's and Jacob's reflections are framed by such a problem-solving approach, and the effectiveness of their adaptations is measured by the usefulness of their chosen pedagogy as a behaviour management strategy. Their priority is to increase their students' on-task behaviours and engagement with the material taught, which they achieve. It is hard to fault this approach, as at least some of the English lesson is spent on its original objective—doing writing—and only part of the lesson is used for other activities—sport or Fear Factor-type activities—that would seem not to have a place in a writing lesson. This is a better outcome than before, when some students might not have produced anything during similar lessons.

However, by prioritising the need for behaviour management, Leanne and Jacob are only able to consider the immediate, short-term effects of the strategies they employ. Although they result in better engagement and participation, the long-term consequences of their choice of strategy on students' lives remain invisible to them. Later in this chapter we will discuss some less immediately obvious consequences and how these can be revealed by applying a particular problematisation framework. Next, however, we consider, in general, why it is important that teacher decision making is informed by a strategy's long-term effects in addition to short-term effectiveness.

In Chapter 2 we showed some of the long-term consequences of teacher strategy choice on students' lives with the example of the special sport class from Saltmarsh and Youdell (2004), who vividly demonstrated how a school's timetabling practices, along with resource and space allocation, created different conditions of possibility for different groups of students. Some students were provided with ideal conditions for skill practice, and as a result they were able to improve their skills. Other student groups were forced to work in an environment that actively prevented them from learning new skills or improving existing ones.

Watkins (2007) has also demonstrated how the pedagogy chosen by teachers during a writing lesson can render "the pedagogic space either more or less conducive to learning" (p. 779) by comparing the writing lessons of two Australian teachers, Narelle and Jane.

Although the students in her study were Year 2—much younger than Jacob's and Leanne's students—her examples are relevant for our purposes.

According to Watkins (2007), Narelle's lesson included a frequent rotation of activities, which involved lots of movement and group work with less time spent on teacher-directed activities. When her students had to work without the proximity of their teacher they found it difficult to discipline themselves. They became unsettled and were unable to curb their physical activities to apply themselves to the writing task. They "tended to be more focused on talking to their friends and only sporadically engaging with the materials" (p. 775). Thus, Narelle's movement-rich writing lesson proved challenging for students who had not yet developed the disposition for academic work. Those who already had the scholarly habit of sitting at their desks could spend more time on task than those without such experience. For them, the lesson simply confirmed existing habits.

Jane, on the other hand, "favoured a regimen that curbed movement and noise and encouraged bodily composure when lessons were in progress" (p. 777). Jane also believed movement was unsettling for the students, so she designed group-based activities that minimised movement and maintained order. Watkins concluded that in Jane's lessons "[s]tudents did not simply acquire a grounding in basic handwriting movements ... but the discipline required for engaging in literate practice" (p. 778). They had a particular composure when writing and could apply themselves to work for sustained periods.

The pedagogies teachers employ not only affect short-term engagement with tasks, they also influence the quality of students' learning and levels of skill acquisition, which have implications for future learning. From the students' perspective it matters how competent or fast they might become in writing, and also whether the writing skills they learn from a young age will enable them to write a submission to the city council, for instance, or an essay in an exam situation. The completion of an exam task might make entrance to tertiary education possible, and higher qualification levels might provide access to more satisfying jobs with higher pay, and so on. Thus students' future possibilities can be indirectly supported or hindered by the practices teachers choose, even with very young children.

Davies (2006) has called the potential future outcomes of various teaching practices "conditions of possibility". Each teaching practice creates certain conditions but not others. Davies suggests that teachers have to ask, "[i]n what ways do those conditions of possibility afford our students a viable life? And in what ways may they be said to fall short of adequate care?" (Davies, 2006, p. 437). Had these questions been available to Leanne and Jacob, they might not have included movement-rich activities in their writing lessons on a regular basis. Instead, they might have found a way of supporting their students through the discomfort of staying still and focusing on their writing, a skill they seem to have found difficult but that was necessary to acquire if they wanted access to tertiary education. Considering the future conditions of possibility particular pedagogies create for students beyond short-term efficacy is especially important when the pressures of immediate responses to ongoing disruptions might prevent such considerations from becoming a high priority.

Jacob and Leanne complement their 'what works' approach to reflection by student preference-driven decision making. They privilege what students want in the moment. They draw on a notion of teaching and the teacher's role that avoids student discomfort and assumes that good pedagogy has to invite only positive emotional responses. If students do not feel good, or if their emotional responses are not positive, it is interpreted as the fault of the pedagogy (see Furedi, 2009) rather than as a possible effect of the underlying assumptions that inform that pedagogy (such as that students must feel good all the time while learning). Therefore, the only response available to teachers is pleasing the students or choosing strategies that will not invite resistance. Their decisions are also influenced by the extent of interest children might have in an activity rather than by their experience and knowledge of those specific skills that will serve the children well in the future.

This kind of student preference-driven decision making is usually privileged by progressive or student-centred pedagogy, which is critical of so-called traditional or teacher-centred pedagogies, qualifying those as repressive. Santoro Gomez (2008) and Watkins (2007) both argue that placing different pedagogies and students' and teachers' interests in a binary opposition is not helpful when responding to conflict, as one member of the binary will always have to be relegated to the margins. In a teacher-centred approach, commonly associated with authoritarian teachers and silenced students, it is the students who are pushed to the margins, out of the centre. By contrast, in a student-centred approach, it is the teacher who is condemned to the periphery. Santoro Gomez (2008) criticises student-centred pedagogy because it marginalises the teacher and misinterprets power as evil. She suggests that authority is necessary for teaching. We agree that equating student-centred notions of pedagogy with liberation and teacher-centred notions with oppression creates a false dichotomy of the roles of teacher and student. Polarising teachers and students by placing them either at the centre or at the margins does not solve relationship problems in the long run. On the contrary, it sets up teachers and students in opposition to one another.

We believe that a pedagogic space should be a dynamic, negotiated and shifting space rather than fixed. However, we do not believe that flexibility should mean the shifting of decision-making power from teacher to students, or vice versa. Such practices are based on a notion of power as a commodity that can be possessed and as repressive and negative. According to such a notion, power is either held or not and can be transferred from one person to the other. In a conceptualisation of power based on Foucault (1980, 1982, 1995, 2000c), power is productive rather than repressive. It produces people's actions more than it prohibits them. This notion of power can help overcome binary oppositions between teachers and students, and also between teaching and relationship strategies. If Jacob and Leanne had been familiar with this constitutive notion of power, they could have considered how the ideas that privileged action and motion over sitting, thinking and writing in an English lesson produced students' resistances to such quiet activities, and how these same ideas created an ongoing demand for something more exciting. Instead of being guided by students' preferences, they would have reflected on the usefulness of these ideas, which might have led to a different course of action. We will say more about this later when we introduce the specific problematisation process that can help analyse the effects of ideas on people's relationships, practices and possibilities.

Analysis

Discourse and discursive practices

We referred to knowledge in the previous chapter as a particular version of how the world should be or a regime of truth that defines what is doable and sayable, and by whom. We also showed how some knowledges might enjoy greater social support, and are thus valued more highly, than other knowledges because they support moral orders privileged by those in power. We referred to the inseparability of knowledge from the exercise of power. In this chapter we expand on the notion of knowledge and introduce the concepts of discourse and power/knowledge. Familiarity with these concepts is necessary for those who want to perform the processes of problematisation we introduce.

> A discourse refers to a set of meanings, metaphors, representations, images, stories, statements and so on that in some way together produce a particular version of events. It refers to a particular picture that is painted of an event (or person or class of persons), a particular way of representing it or them in a certain light. (Burr, 1995, p. 48)

Burr further explains that every person, event or object can be represented by several different discourses, each of which tells a different story about them. Education, learning and the role of teachers and students can all be the objects of several discourses about schooling. The notion of education as a public good and a right of each citizen is one discourse about education. Similarly, there are many different discourses of learning, each describing how effective learning might happen and the responsibilities and rights of teachers and students. Some discourses of learning prescribe obedience to a master, leader or coach who always has more expertise than his/her students. Students are meant to listen and accept without questioning the usefulness of the regime allocated to them by the coach or teacher within this discourse. They are meant to perform what they are instructed to do without resistance. In other words, they are expected to submit to the discourse (Butler, 1995; Davies, 2006) in exchange for mastery of the skills taught.

Martial arts, kapa haka, ballet, swimming and some group sports are often taught in this way. When we observe training sessions in these sports, we can see students disciplining their bodies and performing and practising in unison with what their coach or teacher asks them to do. They usually do not give their opinions, as they would during a discussion in social studies or English, where their opinions might be actively sought by the teacher. The latter interactions are supported by a different discourse of learning, one that privileges student opinion and active contribution, in contrast to the authoritarian approach taken by some sport coaches.

Each discourse enables certain practices while disabling or limiting others. When we observe a class, we can easily identify the practices that teachers and students engage in. However, we seldom think of the, mostly hidden, assumptions without which the practices do not make sense. Foucault (1972, 1980) used the term 'discourse' to denote both a body of *knowledge*, or a subject discipline, such as medicine, psychology or education, and a set of *practices* that, when associated with a particular discipline, form specific objects, strategies and persons in relation to that discipline. Foucault claimed that knowledge is intertwined with power, because it acts upon the actions of individuals (Arribas-Ayllon & Walkerdine, 2008) by creating and withholding "the conditions of possibility of particular lives" (Davies, 2006, p. 436).

A different notion of power

Power/knowledge does not operate in the same way as oppressive power, which is exercised through coercion (Foucault, 2000c). Rather, it is constitutive or productive of practices and identities in ways that enable some things at the expense of others. For example, teacher-centred discourses of schooling privilege the teacher's leadership role, while at the same time constraining the kind of student participation and contribution to decision making that a student-centred pedagogy would allow. Foucault (1980, 2000a, 2000b) also makes a distinction between power as an issue of domination and subordination, and relationships of power. Within an oppressive relationship there is no scope for the oppressed party to change or move, and relationships are frozen. In a relationship of power, however, exercising power involves acting upon another acting subject who can refuse, rebel or choose to comply (Davies, Flemmen, Gannon, Laws, & Watson, 2002, p. 298). Power is not a possession within such a relationship, but more a series of strategies developed by individuals who simultaneously exercise power *and* are affected by it. Thus, power is not unilaterally wielded and neither is it negative and repressive. It is productive, dynamic, shifting and negotiable.

Davies (2005) claims that this kind of productive power, or the power of discourse, can shape practices and relationships in ways that are not immediately obvious, a circumstance that she attributes to what she calls the "seeping into consciousness" quality of power/knowledge. This quality is demonstrated in a story about Nelson Mandela, in which Mandela reacts with some panic to the sight of a black pilot of the plane he is about to board. For a moment he thinks of this person as not being competent enough to fly the plane. However, he catches himself by identifying the discourse through which his anxiety has been produced. In order to counteract this 'seeping into consciousness' quality of discourse, Davies et al. (2002) recommend the use of strategies that shift consciousness by identifying some of the problematic effects of a practice that has become accepted as normal.

Assumptions about teaching and learning and the practices that support them can seep into consciousness in the same way in which racist assumptions occupied Mandela's thoughts. They can then become taken-for-granted 'actions upon the actions' of persons, constituting what will be seen as normal or best-practice solutions. This will also make those assumptions exempt from scrutiny and critique. The problematisation process that we outline shortly is one such consciousness-shifting strategy. It can be applied to everyday teaching practice such as Leanne's and Jacob's accounts of how they teach writing.

Power/knowledge

Each discourse supports different identities and relationship qualities. People construct identities according to available discourses by voluntarily complying with their prescriptions. They then regulate their conduct and behave in accordance with the moral order privileged by a discourse. Each discourse also sets up power relationships between people. Those who accept the moral order a discourse supports will benefit from it, as they will be recognised as an appropriate person within that discourse. Those who act differently might have to struggle to be recognised as normal.

Any discourse, such as a particular notion of schooling, can become dominant when it enjoys social and moral support from those in positions of power within a particular community. Dominant discourses either make other ideas undesirable or may close down access to them altogether (Winslade, 2005). Arribas-Ayllon and Walkerdine (2008) give a detailed account of how this process evolved over the 20th century in relation to student-centred and teacher-centred pedagogies, with student-centred notions gaining ascendancy and teacher-centred pedagogies losing their previous dominant status. Dominant discourses define which identities and relationship practices are considered legitimate and who can be themselves without making an effort to claim their identity and who cannot. A teacher who believes in restorative practices will respond to student misbehaviours differently from a teacher who believes in punishment. He or she will most likely be interested in students' perspectives, while a punitive teacher might not. However, a restorative teacher might find it difficult to perform their preferred identity in a punitive school, where negotiations and conversations with students would not be supported. The world views that are accepted as normal and that enjoy the moral support of those in power often define the culture of a place. This explains why some schools are considered restorative while others are seen as punitive.

We have already talked about how moral orders can be maintained through habitual citations; in other words, by repetitive performances of the same actions, behaviours and ways of relating. The dominance of discourses, and the hidden assumptions that support them, are also maintained by repetitive performances of the practices that these ideas call into being. Often these repetitive performances—or habitual citations—maintain a status quo that serves the interests of powerful groups and alliances. If this natural order of things remains unchallenged, then power relationships can become fixed and frozen. Foucault (2000c) warns that fixed power relationships can turn into a state of domination, in which the oppressed party has no scope for movement or action. In Deleuze and Guattari's (1987) terms, a smooth space becomes more striated. Because of this, Foucault emphasises the importance of critiquing and problematising existing power relationships. We will now turn to introducing a simple process of doing just that.

Problematisation: 'troubling' the power of ideas and making what is too easy harder

The process of problematisation is described by Foucault (1981) in the following statement:

> A critique does not consist in saying that things aren't good the way they are. It consists in seeing on what type of assumptions, of familiar notions, of established, unexamined ways of thinking the accepted practices are based ... To do criticism is to make harder those acts which are now too easy. (p. 456)

But how might one make acts that are too easy, or have become accepted as the natural order of things, harder? Foucault (1972, 1981) invites us to reverse what is seen as the natural order by normalising what is considered problematic, while making undesirable the practice that was previously considered normal. This move opens up a different perspective, making it possible to examine a practice from within a different regime of truth, one that might not have been available previously. The purpose of such problematisation is not to offer solutions, nor to decide the value of a practice by considering whether it is effective in producing certain outcomes. Nor is it carried out to support conclusions about a person's worth or place in the social hierarchy. Problematisation can, however, expose some of the hidden assumptions that make a practice seem rational and reasonable (Davies et al., 2002) and bring into conscious awareness the practices that those same assumptions marginalise and keep hidden. Next, we apply this reversal process to the specific teaching practices of Leanne and Jacob.

From Jacob's and Leanne's accounts of how they modified their English lessons, it appears that both worked hard to find a strategy to at once stop behavioural disruptions and student resistance and lead to increased engagement with writing. They both worked to constitute themselves as responsible and caring practitioners, aware of the effects of their practices for their students. They listened to students' responses and incorporated their knowledge of students into their decision making. They identified and rejected strategies they had found to be ineffective and selected instead strategies they considered more responsive to their students' needs. Jacob dismissed sitting down and analysing texts, saying that "It was pointless for me to sit down, because, you know, sitting down with those boys and giving them texts and read this and try and analyse it, just doesn't work". Leanne concluded that it was important to provide exciting experiences immediately before the students were asked to write because motivation improved and "They want to write about something straight after it has happened, not a week later." Both teachers demonstrated not only knowledge of their students but also knowledge of the teaching as inquiry cycle recommended in *The New Zealand Curriculum* (Ministry of Education, 2007, p. 35). Both worked to constitute themselves as professionals who employed effective pedagogy. In other words, Jacob and Leanne applied what Foucault (2000a) calls "technologies of the self", and they regulated their own conduct "by acting on themselves within a particular moral order and according to a more or less conscious ethical goal" (Arribas-Ayllon & Walkerdine, 2008, p. 103).

Knowledges or discourses are productive of persons' identities and they privilege certain practices while disabling others (Davies, 2006; Foucault, 1972, 1980). It is possible to trace, in persons' accounts of their practices, the knowledges they tap into when they constitute themselves as competent subjects. When Jacob and Leanne work to stop behaviour problems in order to engage their students with writing, they also draw on a number of educational discourses to inform their decision making. Leanne demonstrates familiarity with learning styles (Gardner, 2006), commenting that "Kids are much more tactile these days." Jacob uses knowledge relating to boys' education and of the claims that boys need different strategies from girls (Biddulph, 2008) when he concludes, "You know, sitting down with those boys and giving them texts and read this and try and analyse it, just doesn't work. They dismiss it as boring." Both teachers align themselves with a student-centred pedagogy (Watkins, 2007). Instead of acting from an authoritarian position of expertise, they consider their students' preferences and deliver them the 'good stuff' because, as Leanne says, "They expect it. If you want good stuff out of them you've got to do good stuff with them first."

However, these same educational discourses, which invite Jacob and Leanne to dismiss 'sitting down', 'texts' and 'analysing' as boring and unsuitable practices for their students, invite them to accept the action-packed activity they provide at the start of their writing lesson as an effective strategy. *Play* becomes a standard for good pedagogy ("We do sport and recreation as part of their English group, so we go and play a sport and do something"), rather than something that 13–14-year-olds might do outside school. Arribas-Ayllon and Walkerdine (2008) provide a historical overview of how ideas that oppose coercion, such as individual freedom and self-government, have contributed to the emergence of play as a site of learning, which also requires teachers "to observe, monitor and intervene in the development of the child by accurately reading their actions" (p. 97). Jacob and Leanne do just that, while avoiding conflict with their students.

A different approach from problem solving, one that unpacks the very ideas that inform the practices taken for granted by Jacob and Leanne as good pedagogy, will produce a different outcome. In the following we demonstrate how the practice of playing during an English lesson and the provision of 'Fear Factor' activities can be critiqued and troubled somewhat.

Jacob rejects as pointless "sitting down", "giving them texts" and "read this and try and analyse it" because his students dismiss these as boring. Leanne starts her lesson with tactile activities that involve movement ("I made up all this goo and blindfolded them"), and she believes in the necessity of providing such experiences immediately before her students are required to write. It is the bodily discipline of staying carpentered to a desk and committing thoughts from memory onto paper that the two teachers render problematic through their choice of activities. When a practice is rejected and problematised in this way, as sitting down is in this case, it is its binary opposition, doing "sport and recreation" and "Fear Factor type of stuff", that manages to stay invisible and exempt from scrutiny (Davies, 1998).

So does free movement and not having to make an effort to remember events from the past. None of these practices get discussed and reflected on, because, as Foucault (1980) would say, they have become the natural order of things. It is this unnoticed and undiscussed 'natural order' that becomes accepted as good practice and that is unavailable for analysis. A Foucauldian critique invites us to reverse this order by normalising what is seen as problematic and by problematising what is considered normal (see Arribas-Ayllon & Walkerdine, 2008, for a step-by-step demonstration of Foucauldian analysis). By privileging an action-packed lead-up to their writing lesson, Jacob and Leanne—most likely unintentionally—also reject the practice of controlling the body by reducing movement and sitting down. As a result, they also reduce the time available for writing.

One could say that Jacob and Leanne are doing everything right from their students' perspective. Yet the question remains whether they can secure the students' ongoing collaboration and compliance with the writing task. Leanne's statement that "Next week I'm going to take them out and do bubbles" suggests that she anticipates the recurrence of the problem of defiance unless she continues to provide sufficient excitement. It is the teachers who continue to work hard 'to do good stuff', while the students' responsibility for and contribution to the learning process remains undiscussed. While Jacob's and Leanne's chosen pedagogy reduces disruptive behaviours and their students engage with the learning tasks temporarily, the actual time spent on writing is reduced, and, for part of the lesson at least, the conditions that help students practise the bodily discipline of writing are withheld. Yet this is exactly the competency the students need to develop.

Focusing on what might be the most effective strategy solves the urgent problem of behaviour management, but the long-term, unintended consequences of an otherwise good pedagogy remain unnoticed and unchallenged by the teachers. The very pedagogy that enables behaviour management also disables, or reduces the time spent on, the development of a key competency. These contradictory effects demonstrate the paradoxical doubleness of discursive practices (Davies, 2006). It is always easier to notice the enabling effects of any practice—in this case the reduction of behaviour problems—while the negative consequences of a practice might remain elusive and not immediately obvious. A reflection process informed by Foucault's ideas about critique can shift attention away from the immediate efficacy of practice onto less obvious but potentially harmful long-term effects on students' possibilities.

When teachers analyse their practices in this way during discussions with colleagues, they can more easily problematise what is taken for granted and normalise what might be seen as problematic by students during an interaction. They can ask a question on the spot that invites students to think about the effects of ideas on their behaviour or on interactions with others, or have longer conversations with their students later, during a class meeting. In the next chapter we introduce a class meeting process that supports a collaborative examination of unhelpful ideas by teachers and students.

Here is a list of some possible questions for students to consider that Jacob and Leanne came up with after performing the above problematisation. They bring to the students' conscious awareness the very practices that were dismissed initially by Jacob and Leanne. The questions invite students to consider the usefulness or 'normality' of what was previously rendered problematic, such as sitting, practising, engaging in writing, versus sport and play, or stillness versus movement. It would not have been possible to normalise these practices in this way without the problematisation process described previously:

> What kind of activities will help you become better at writing?
>
> In what ways could sitting down and focusing on what you might write help you come up with a good story?
>
> How might reading others' stories and looking at what they have done support your own story writing?
>
> Is the expectation that teachers should provide interesting and action-packed activities in every writing lesson realistic?
>
> How is moving around and doing sport helpful to think about your topic?

The problematisation process that was applied to these two teachers' choice of pedagogy in response to recurring student resistance during writing lessons does not offer generalisable conclusions and permanent solutions to how classroom disruptions can be reduced to better engage students with learning. Neither does it offer conclusions about the quality of the two teachers' literacy programme. The process can, however, interrupt the repeated validation and inscription of privileged assumptions and pedagogies—in this case action-packed language experiences—as normal and *always* useful for *all* students. It can also keep as an option, and show the benefits of, a pedagogy—in this case, the disciplining of the body—that might otherwise be rendered problematic and rejected as a useful choice. The phrase, 'disciplining of the body' derives from Foucault's comments on how power works through discourse to produce practices. The value of thinking about teaching practice in this way is that it can keep both the privileged and the marginalised practices of a binary opposition in conscious awareness and admissible into professional debates. It shows how "[b]inary divisions systematically disadvantage one half of each binary" (Davies, 1996, p. 12).

Challenging the superiority of one half of a binary offers a *both/and* rather than an *either/or* stance, which can keep the debate open and facilitate reflection, not only on the advantages of an accepted practice, but also on its constraints and potential disadvantages for some students. This kind of problematisation invites teachers to ask about the "conditions of possibility" (Davies, 2006) a chosen practice affords to students beyond the classroom and beyond its short-term effectiveness in a few lessons. The process might also prompt us to ask, in this example, whether movement-rich, experiential activities serve those students well who do not come to school with "the necessary training of the body for academic labour" (Watkins, 2007, p. 774), and whose parents are unable to provide such training. Is what might seem the best pedagogy in the moment also the best pedagogy for all students in the long run?

Summary of main points in Chapter 5

- Previous chapters have introduced conversational moves that reduce the effects of exclusion.
- This chapter addresses how to challenge ideas in the social context that exclude, oppress or disadvantage students.
- A process of problematisation can help generate alternative pedagogies.
- A discourse is a set of meanings that produces a set of events.
- Each discourse enables some practices and disables others.
- Discourses are intertwined with regimes of power.
- Power/knowledge has the ability to seep into consciousness.
- Teacher and student practices are supported by discourses about schooling.
- Prioritising behaviour management can produce short-term results at the expense of long-term learning benefits.

- Potential future outcomes of various teaching practices produce 'conditions of possibility'.
- We need to ask, 'In what ways do those conditions of possibility afford students a viable life?'
- Pedagogies are usually shaped by either teacher-centred or student-centred discourses.
- Discourses are troubled by problematisation of practices that appear to be the natural order.
- This troubling involves normalising what appears problematic and problematising what seems normal.

Figure 5: Problematising discourses of teaching and learning

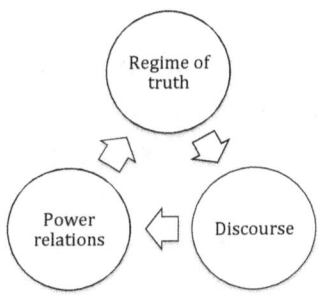

When...
A discourse excludes, oppresses or disadvantages students, it can be troubled, unsettled, deconstructed, problematised

How do conditions of possibility afford students a viable life?

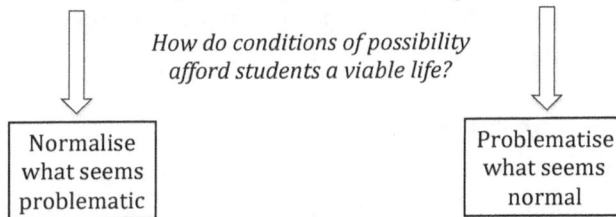

Exercise

Discourses are statements that describe an object. We have listed a few statements below that we have heard from teachers and students. Each statement implicitly includes an assumption about what a good teacher, student or pedagogy might be. Try to answer each of the following questions in relation to each statement.

- What discourse of schooling does the following statement describe?
- What teacher practices does this statement support or normalise?
- What practices does it render problematic?
- What kind of teacher identities does this statement call into being?
- What student identities would do well in a school where this is the dominant notion of schooling?
- How do students learn best, according to this discourse?
- What teacher strategies and student behaviours support the (re-)production of the kind of school discourse that this statement refers to?

1. Teachers are there to teach subjects. They are not meant to be social workers.
2. Parents have to teach their children how to behave.
3. It is possible to motivate students by making every lesson fun.
4. As a teacher you have to cater for the individual needs of every single child in your classroom.
5. A teacher should be available if a student needs someone to listen to them.
6. Students who use physical violence towards other students have no place in a regular school.
7. Students who do not have good role models at home are less likely to behave appropriately at school.

Questions for reflection
Collect statements from your school that represent discourses of learning that position teachers and students in conflict with each other. Perform a process of problematisation on those ideas similar to the one introduced in this chapter and the exercise.

Chapter 6 A deconstructive approach to class meetings: "There is too much talking. We get very little work done"

Introduction

In the previous chapter we showed how teachers can problematise practices that have become accepted as good pedagogy in order to think differently. We also showed how, in the long run, routine practices might disadvantage students by creating unreasonable student expectations and by normalising notions of learning that are impossible to comply with in every lesson. If these effects are left unchallenged they can contribute to the maintenance of problem behaviours.

In this chapter we show how teachers can facilitate similar thinking and reflection for students about learning or relationship practices either inside or outside the classroom. We introduce a specific format of circle conversation that can be used to structure class meetings, where teachers and students can collaboratively examine popular ideas that work against a classroom culture conducive to learning.

Discourse is also a central concept in this chapter, along with a specific process of deconstruction (White, 1992). The class meeting format we introduce, like the particular problematisation described in the previous chapter, can initiate discussion about practices, behaviours and attitudes which are pushed out of conscious awareness or discarded as unhelpful by dominant ideas. Again, we argue for a way of thinking about relationship practice that goes beyond binary oppositions and an either positive or negative qualification of a practice. Rather, we propose that teaching and relationship practices can have multiple and often contradictory effects. However, these can only be considered by reflecting on their usefulness, or otherwise, in different situations and for different student groups. By using the deconstructive class meeting process that we recommend, teachers can raise questions that stimulate different thinking in students about classroom practices, notions of schooling and ways of interacting. Such a reflection process is what Foucault had in mind, we suspect, when he wrote:

> Thought is not what inhabits a certain conduct and gives it meaning; rather, it is what allows one to step back from this way of acting or reacting, to present it to oneself as an object of thought and to question it as to its meaning, its conditions, and its goals. Thought is freedom in relation to what one does, the motion by which one detaches oneself from it, establishes it as an object, and reflects on it as a problem. (Foucault, cited in Rabinow, 2000, p. xxxv).

"It is hard for teachers to teach us and we can't learn"

The staff and some students of a multicultural school had repeatedly expressed their concerns about the negative impact on the learning culture of minor, but ongoing, disruptions and conflicts. They were also concerned about "unjustified meanness", which they said had been manifested as talking over others, interrupting and not waiting for one's turn, and bullying those who followed teachers' instructions. Students who observed school rules were often called "nerds" or "teachers' pets" by bullies. Their appearance or clothing was also criticised and ridiculed. If they continued to 'please' the teachers, at times they were sworn at and even threatened with physical violence. Some teachers believed that the bullying of teachers—blatantly disregarding instructions, or of them as persons—was also on the rise, contaminating and suppressing the positive learning culture the school had maintained for a long time. All these behaviours interfered with teaching and learning.

The teachers tried various behaviour modification strategies, such as rewarding students who were on task and giving after-school detentions to those who were not (which usually involved picking up rubbish around the school campus, cleaning a classroom, or doing some other service for the school). They also taught assertiveness to victims of bullying and referred the students who bullied to behaviour specialist teachers, who taught them social skills. Some of the bullies were sent to the school counsellor. Several teachers, along with the school counsellors, believed that if these students reflected on and examined the effects of their behaviours on others they would develop empathy, which in turn would compel them to stop bullying behaviours. However, these interventions only brought about temporary changes. They did not eliminate the behaviours that stressed several teachers and students.

Some teachers became quite distressed about this state of affairs, as they felt unable to establish the order necessary for them to teach. Teachers who were at the receiving end of disrespectful behaviours more than others became especially disheartened and were contemplating leaving their jobs. They were told by senior managers to toughen up and to learn more classroom management strategies. Students who wanted to learn also complained about the distractions they had to put up with. They said they did not get any work done and it was hard for their teachers to teach because of the students who did not want to learn and were disrespectful towards both their teachers and their peers. Some of these students were contemplating enrolling at another school.

The staff agreed that, in addition to finding effective ways of addressing interruptions to lessons and bullying, there was a need to develop more respectful relationships between students and between teachers and students. Strengthening relationships within classrooms was hypothesised by a majority of teachers to reduce both the number of interruptions to teaching and learning, and bullying behaviours.

Analysis

Individualised interventions

In New Zealand the quality of teacher–student relationships has been shown to directly correlate with students' achievement levels, especially for indigenous Māori (Bishop, Berryman, Tiakiwai, & Richardson,

2003) and students from low socio-economic backgrounds (Hill & Hawk, 2005). Bishop, Berryman, Cavanagh and Teddy (2006) found that all students' assessment results significantly improved when teachers made minor changes to their practices, which included, among other things, showing an interest in or trying to better understand students' perspectives. By contrast, when teachers did not make an effort to engage with students on a personal level, students demonstrated fewer learning behaviours.

When teachers respond to disruptions, non-compliance, defiance and bullying behaviours, often triggered by tensions in the teacher–student relationship, they have a variety of strategies to choose from. Behaviour management, social skill training and various anti-bullying programmes are particularly popular because they provide replicable strategies and interventions. We do not completely dismiss behavioural approaches to conflict (see, for example, Rogers, 2002, 2011). These approaches are teacher-centred in the sense that they rely on the external control of student behaviours by the teacher, but they can be useful in situations when there is little time for negotiation and the flow of the lesson has to be maintained. However, such behaviour management programmes, along with social skill training, are also highly individualised and locate problems in particular individual students who disrupt lessons or bully others. Subsequently, these individual students are seen to be in need of training and intervention in order to change. Yet a meta-analysis of anti-bullying programmes concluded that there is little evidence that they produce lasting changes or eliminate bullying permanently (Galloway & Roland, 2004).

The teachers in our example used such individualised interventions with particular students. Our preference, however, is for interventions that address the relational dynamics of the group, and also address ideas and practices circulating in the social context that endorse, and thus maintain, disrespect. We believe that students' relationship competencies can be more efficiently developed if teachers use approaches that endorse a *working with* rather than a *doing to* philosophy of addressing disruptions to lessons, conflict and bullying. Such interventions can also suitably complement schools' projects of inclusion and citizenship education. Conflict resolution and community building are two possible approaches of particular interest to us.

Increasingly, schools in New Zealand are using various adaptations of restorative practice processes for preventive purposes and daily relationship management, in addition to responding to relationship breakdowns. Many teachers draw on the work of prominent restorative practitioners, who provide a wide range of examples (Costello, Wachtel, & Wachtel, 2010; Hopkins, 2004, 2011; Restorative Practices Development Team, 2004; Thorsborne & Vinegrad, 2007; Winslade & Williams, 2012). Most recently, the Ministry of Education has made it possible for a large number of schools to receive training in restorative practices within their PB4L (Positive Behaviour for Learning) initiative.

In this chapter we focus on how circle conversations can be adapted from restorative practice as one strategy for responding to ongoing relationship trouble. In contrast to individual interventions, circle conversations offer a framework for problematisation and collaborative problem solving between teachers and students. They engage groups and classroom communities in reflecting on the effects of different behaviours on others, while supporting students to clarify their stance on relationship practices. We will show the potential of circle conversations as the basis for daily relationship management and a strategy for establishing a positive learning culture in a classroom.

Circle conversations

Circle conversations, or circles, have been utilised in the classroom for multiple purposes, including community building, conflict resolution and subject teaching (Costello et al., 2010). Although there are many traditions of talking in circles, the modern practice of circle conversations in classrooms is recognised as originating in indigenous cultures in North America. It also bears many similarities to a Māori hui. The specific format of circles we introduce is designed to combine community building with responding to relationship problems. Before describing this format in more detail, we will highlight some characteristics of circle conversations that distinguish them from other meetings.

Most commonly used meeting formats, in educational and other organisational settings, are structured by the agenda items, procedure and length of time allocated to the meeting. This means that participants can freely offer their contributions whenever they feel like it, depending on their confidence, knowledge of the topic and willingness to offer a perspective. In the absence of mechanisms that set out to equalise the length and frequency of a person's contributions, at least to some extent, many meetings turn into forums dominated by the monologues of one or only a few persons, which also limits the exchange of different and contradictory ideas and arguments between all participants. Some people can feel totally silenced or scared to contribute, especially when a meeting is controlled by persons who occupy positions higher in the social hierarchy of the organisation. This was the case for Kate, the young teacher in our example in Chapter 2, who had a different opinion about Harry from her deputy principal. She felt a need to censor her contributions in staff meetings. Those meetings reinscribed existing power relationships between staff members.

Circle conversations interrupt habitual ways of engaging and interacting with others and thus often achieve very different outcomes from traditional meeting formats, such as approval of a suggestion or decision by a majority vote. Circles can rework, rather than reinscribe, existing power relationships through the responses to differences that they make possible.

First, the meeting space is utilised differently to enable a different quality of engagement with others. Rearranging the classroom and asking students and teachers to sit in a circle and for each participant to take turns to contribute has both practical and philosophical applications. This spatial arrangement provides a structure that regulates discussion, requiring students and teachers to act and think differently from their usual ways of interacting. Practically, a circle allows all participants to see and hear each other; therefore, no one can hide. The control of contributions by facilitators requires everyone to voice their views without interruptions and equalises the number of contributions each participant can make. It thus demands that teachers and influential and vocal students become listeners, while quiet students can speak without interruption. The contributions of students who might otherwise be silenced are brought forward and the dominance of teachers and powerful students is reduced. Initially some might find this shift difficult and it takes time to become comfortable with the process. However, the sharing of everyone's perspectives can help the appreciation of differences and prevent some views from becoming dominant.

Circle conversations facilitate intra-action

Another characteristic of the circle format is that it can create an *intra-active flow* (Barad, 2003, 2007), which supports participants to be open to affect and to be affected by others. What does this mean? Hamilton and Kecskemeti (2015) found that using circle conversations in tertiary education with prospective teachers for the discussion of sensitive issues relating to inclusion and exclusion reduced the frequency of destructive emotional responses that had previously been common. The circle structure supported the admissability into the discussion of individual differences and participants' previously unspoken personal experiences; for example, narratives about family members who had a disability, and often painful personal experiences of exclusion. Instead of questioning the relevance of such narratives, or moralising and judging others, participants were often moved by the stories they heard. Subsequently they started reflecting on their own assumptions about social differences and normative requirements. Conducting discussions in circles thus generated the kinds of shifts in consciousness we referred to in the previous chapter and opened up new ways of thinking about difference (Deleuze & Guattari, 1987). In other words, transformative moments were achieved, during which participants were mutually affecting each other in a series of movements, in contrast to previous occasions when they reacted negatively to each other's categorial differences.

The theoretical concept of *intra-action*, in contrast with the notion of *interaction*, can illuminate why circle conversations can invite such different modes of engagement. Openness to being affected by each other, and by new ideas, is what Barad (2003) refers to as *intra*-action. Rather than two separate entities interacting with each other, those who engage intra-actively affect, and are open to being affected by, the other.

In contrasting the two concepts of interaction and intra-action, Davies and Gannon (2012) suggest that interaction is an exchange between separate, pre-existing entities and individual agencies. During such an exchange, difference is held as a fixed, categorial attribute that creates distance, rather than connection between people. People respond to others in terms of categorial distinctions—as males and not females, as

European and not Māori, as able-bodied and not disabled. In an interaction, a claim to membership of a category group provides the dominant terms of engagement through which one encounters the other.

Intra-action, on the other hand, re-envisages the encounter between persons as an entanglement of agencies, where each mutually affects the other in an ongoing series of movements. Beings are actually, despite their best efforts, "always entangled and always becoming something other than they were" (Davies & Gannon 2012, p. 361). The concept of intra-action exposes the underlying instability and fluidity of categories, with difference continuing to emerge as a product of "the movement generated in an encounter, in which two or more bodies are in a process of becoming different" (p. 361). Through the process of becoming "open to becoming different from themselves" (Davies, 2009, p. 19), particular ways of being and categories that delineate the participants are transformed.

Circles establish a different temporary alignment between people. They create an assemblage by arranging both the spatial location and the mode of engagement of participants (Davies & Gannon, 2012). They bring together bodies, thoughts, feelings and experiences in ways that can generate the kind of movement in which each participant can become different from what they were before. This temporary alignment creates an affective climate, which increases participants' capacity to "*affect* and to be *affected*" (Davies & Gannon, 2012, p. 369, emphasis in original).

Teaching children to think

We think circle conversations also provide a forum for performing the kind of critique Butler (2004a) recommends. She suggests that to critique is to question our most sure ways of knowing, which is another way of describing the troubling of taken-for-granted or habitual ways of doing and being. The problematisation process introduced in Chapter 5 is thus also a form of critique. Butler says we should perform critique when there is a crisis, when traditional categories and concepts cannot describe adequately what is happening. In such instances, critique can make visible the nature of a problem and, further, can open up possibilities for action for consideration. Critique also opens up the space to question, without censure, the particular *forms* governmentality is taking. It asks why "be governed *like that*, by that, in the name of those principles, with such and such an objective in mind and by means of such procedures, not like that, not for that, not by them" (Butler, 2004a, p. 312, emphasis in original).

In another application of circle conversations, this time with counselling practitioners, Kecskemeti and Hamilton (2015) found that the particular assemblage afforded by circles, and the participants' openness to being affected by others' narratives of their lived experience, was able to surface commonalities of practitioners' experiences. They could identify a recurring pattern in the stories shared: finding paid employment and being able to accumulate the required number of hours for registration with their professional organisation was a systemic, rather than an individual, problem. This recognition opened up the space to consider whether they should accept the available systems of transitioning from training through registration to practice and paid employment, or should contemplate the possibilities of collective action that might change existing systems.

Is this notion of critique relevant to relationship problems in the classroom? When teacher–student or student–student relationships are not going well and it is impossible to teach and to learn, we can say that there is a crisis. In those instances, teachers and students could examine together how particular discourses of schooling and learning govern the actions of students and teachers in ways that are not immediately obvious. After such an examination they can choose to question or accept the forms of governmentality these discourses support.

Ongoing bullying by some students, or by teachers, of other students is one such crisis that calls for critique, or, as Davies (2011a) suggests, highlights the need for teaching children to think, instead of responding to bullying by teaching social skills to individual students. The class meeting format we introduce in this chapter can be used as a process of critique, which, at the same time:

> enables children to learn new *skills of thinking* about social justice and about the parts they play in creating it; it opens up the chance for children to *develop their* own *social and ethical positions* in relation to others and in relation to difference. (Davies, 2011a, p. 279, emphasis in original)

Individualised interventions that focus on skill teaching do not address the ideas and "forms of governmentality" that maintain relationship problems. Neither do they invite students to think about those ideas and to articulate their position in relation to them. Involving students in the collaborative examination of discourses, through a process of problematisation similar to that described in the previous chapter, can help them to develop their own social and ethical positions. We now turn to describing how it can be done in practice.

Deconstruction as a relationship strategy of critique

Our specific deconstructive approach to class meetings builds on an earlier project by The Restorative Practices Development Team (2004), who developed conference, class meeting and interview processes that drew on Māori hui (meeting) protocols (Macfarlane, 2004), constructionist theorising (Burr, 2003) and narrative therapy (White & Epston, 1990). Their work has been inspirational for the design of the particular meeting format that we propose.

Kecskemeti (2011) identified some discourses of learning and notions of schooling as complicit in producing teacher–student conflict. She also found that when teachers collectively deconstructed those discourses, their stress levels reduced and they were able to come up with alternative relationship practices that did not produce conflict. Deconstruction also helped formulate questions that invited students to think about the ideas that maintain conflict. Kecskemeti's findings encourage teachers to *listen*, not only *to* what students and teachers have to say about their conflicts, but also *for* discourses of learning during class meetings.

What distinguishes deconstructive class meetings from other forms of circle conversation is the attention paid to discourses and the frequent, strategic use of deconstructive questioning at various points in the meeting. We have drawn on Foucault's work and his notions of power (Foucault, 1980; Ransom, 1997) to support our argument for giving such a significant role to deconstruction. In addition to oppressive or sovereign power, which involves the use of hostile forces to coercively regulate the conduct of others (Rabinow, 2000), Foucault described another type of power, which he termed productive and constitutive of identities (Davies, 2006; Foucault, 2000a, 2000b). We have referred to this notion of power in the previous chapter, and it is particularly relevant for the approach to conversation with classroom communities.

Unlike oppressive power, which is visible because it is exercised through some form of coercion, productive power operates through the use of knowledge or discourse, according to which persons shape their own conduct in order to take up a particular type of identity. While oppressive power might be easy to spot, productive power is harder to notice, because it operates in hidden ways. We referred to this in Chapter 5, when we recalled how Mandela's thinking was hijacked by racist ideas. Consequently, productive power requires a different intervention from trying to change the visible conduct of persons. What needs to be done instead is to expose the discourses or rationalities that make a particular practice or behaviour seem reasonable and inevitable (Davies et al., 2002; Davies et al., 2006). We believe that the ideas of schooling that teachers and students might use to take up their identities can at times work to undermine their collaboration—against their best intentions. Therefore, the form of circle conversation that we developed consciously sets out to "identify and name the ideas that shape teacher–student, teacher–parent and other relationships in schools, including the ideas that produce antagonistic and disrespectful relationships" (Drewery & Kecskemeti, 2010, p. 110).

How can such a conceptualisation of power be used in a class meeting, and how can the power of discourses be deconstructed or unsettled? When we observe teacher–student interactions in a classroom, the behaviours of both teachers and students are obvious. It is more difficult to identify what discourses or knowledges of schooling inform the practices they engage in and shape the meanings they make of their respective roles. We might see a teacher who clearly defines the boundaries of acceptable and unacceptable behaviour and corrects students who cross those boundaries. We might see students who respond to these corrections without resistance and do what their teacher asks. Both teacher and students may follow the same unwritten rules of interaction, which could be articulated as, 'Teachers decide what happens in the classroom,' and, 'Students have to follow their teachers' instructions all the time.' The teacher–student interaction goes well because neither of them questions these rules. We could say that both teacher and students take up their identities from the same discourse of schooling and both accept the structure of rights and responsibilities that this discourse or rationality prescribes.

However, when students question the tasks set by their teacher—with back-chatting, calling out or swearing—and might say things like, 'I talk because it is boring', or, 'It is your job to teach us', then their behaviours are likely to be informed by ideas that support resistance to activities perceived to be boring and excuse disruptive behaviours. These same ideas might also disable acceptance of either the teacher's leadership role, or the learner's responsibilities (or both), in the teaching and learning interaction. These behaviours are authorised by different beliefs about schooling, such as, 'Learning should be fun,' and, 'Good teachers make all learning activities entertaining,' or, 'Learning is the teacher's responsibility'.

These ideas can also set up a problematic power relationship between teacher and student. If a student enters interactions with teachers with the expectation that they will be entertained on every occasion, then it is very likely they will be disappointed. It is unreasonable to expect all learning activities to be turned into fun and learners not to have to do anything in order to learn a new skill. This idea enables students to resist hard work, persistence and monotonous practice, even when such practice might be necessary to become good at, for example, playing a musical instrument, speaking a foreign language or converting a try in rugby. The same idea also enables constant negative critique of a teacher if she or he does not provide entertainment.

Such discourses or views of schooling have the power to produce particular student and teacher identities, with concomitant behaviours, while suppressing others. Deconstructive questioning can help uncover and unsettle the *power* of a strongly held but unhelpful idea through drawing attention to its opposite (Davies, 1996). In the case of 'fun', discussions can be invited about the usefulness of work or effort. In the case of the idea 'Learning is the teacher's responsibility', a conversation can be started about the respective roles and responsibilities of both teachers and students. A teacher skilled in deconstructive questioning can ask students to reflect on the usefulness or otherwise of particular ideas of learning, as opposed to arguing which idea should be accepted as 'the truth'. The focus is not on the behaviours of students or teachers, but on how specific notions of learning might shape and 'govern' those behaviours.

Questions such as, 'How much practice do you think you might need to invest in learning this skill?' or, 'Do you think it is possible to learn a new skill or concept with only your teacher demonstrating it but without any input from you?' problematise these commonly held ideas, which, we believe, produce conflict between teachers and students. Such questions are not about creating binaries by deciding which notion of schooling or successful learning is better than the other. Rather, deconstructive questions unsettle the dominance of an idea by introducing a plurality of meanings (Davies, 1998) and by showing how binary oppositions always privilege one side of the binary.

Such deconstructive questions, posed in class meetings, invite both students and teachers to evaluate the relational effects of different ideas of learning. They help students and teachers to clarify their positions on particular views of schooling and the roles of teacher and student. This process also supports the questioning of the specific form of governmentality that a particular notion of schooling enables. Such an evaluation is necessary for deciding which notions of schooling and relationship practice to accept or reject. Only after clarifying their own stance does it become easier for teachers and students to negotiate which ideas will produce the kinds of relationship that produce respect and are conducive to teaching and learning. Deconstruction used in class meetings thus supports a critical examination of the advantages and disadvantages of the various discourses that influence teacher–student interactions in a particular class.

A deconstructive approach to class meetings

The particular circle conversation, which is termed a *deconstructive class meeting*, was developed with teachers in a multicultural secondary school in New Zealand, over 3 years, as part of a restorative practices project (Kecskemeti, Kaveney, Gray, & Drewery, 2013). With the help of funding from the Ministry of Education, about 60 teachers at the school volunteered to embark on learning specific theoretical concepts—including the productive power of language, discourse, power/knowledge, normalisation, categorisation—and the ways of speaking and conversational moves adapted from *narrative therapy*—including externalising, (re-)positioning and deconstructive questioning—introduced so far in previous chapters.

The meeting process they collaboratively developed over 3 years was designed to meet two objectives: strengthen the classroom community, and replace problematic relationship patterns with more respectful alternatives. Therefore, every class meeting began with a mixer or relationship-building round, which helped develop new relational dynamics. Teachers were aware that students in secondary schools often become very busy under exam and assessment pressures. During such times, opportunities for connecting with others on a personal level can be diminished. Therefore, they decided to make the most of occasions when class meetings were called and space was provided to pay more than just fleeting attention to others. Nickolite and Doll (2008) claim that "strategies that promote highly effective peer interactions can be instrumental in creating a soothing and supportive social environment that makes it possible for students to stay engaged in academic learning" (p. 103). Hopkins (2011) suggests that "Nobody feels safe if they are surrounded by strangers"(p. 49). Short activities that build and strengthen relationships can also increase feelings of trust and safety, both prerequisites for addressing conflict.

Creating opportunities for participants to connect with peers and teachers they would not otherwise engage with on a personal level relaxes the atmosphere. Starting with connection activities can also make the meetings more inviting for Māori and Pasifika students, whose cultural traditions of meeting protocols include a mihi, or introduction, at the start. Through participants sharing something about themselves, an atmosphere of trust is created, which helps everyone ease into the more serious conflict resolution part of the meeting (Restorative Practices Development Team, 2004). The class meeting also provided opportunities to directly teach the key competencies that had been introduced in *The New Zealand Curriculum* (Ministry of Education, 2007).

The narrative framework helps locate problems in the relationship dynamics rather than in individuals. Another way of saying this is that problems are assumed to originate in events rather than in identity categories (Deleuze, 1990). Drawing on the work of Winslade and Williams (2012), deconstructive class meetings aim to centralise and address "the whole nexus of relationships within a classroom" (p. 111), in contrast to focusing on particular relationships or individual students or teachers. When problems are considered to be "a function of the relationships among the whole group" (p. 113), rather than of individuals, more productive and constructive responses to conflict become available. For the teachers addressing the "whole nexus of relationships" meant that they had to be prepared to give up their familiar ways of addressing conflict, such as dishing out consequences and withdrawing privileges. Like the students, teachers also had to be willing to replace familiar patterns of interaction with ones that re-positioned everyone in relation to others.

Format of class meetings

Pre-meeting tasks

Organisation
Class meetings are commonly called when a class is struggling with learning or teacher–student or student–student relationships and other methods, such as behaviour management, have been ineffective in achieving positive relational outcomes for those concerned. Usually, several teachers of the same class, or in some instances a group of students, suggest that a class meeting be called to discuss concerns and find a way forward. In the lead-up to a class meeting, the teachers of a particular class share their concerns and discuss their hopes for a meeting. If students want to call a meeting, they will first talk to their form teacher or dean.

When a number of teachers experience difficulties with the same group, or a significant number of students are unhappy with how things are in their class, usually subject teachers, the form teacher and the dean of that year level will all attend one or more consecutive meetings with the same class. When a series of meetings is deemed necessary, each subject teacher of the class gives up a lesson to ensure that students do not miss more than one lesson in any one subject. Relievers are organised, where possible, but teachers often give up their non-contact time or exchange relief to support each other. They do this in the belief that the time invested in strengthening a classroom community will be compensated for by the increase in caring and on-task behaviours.

Roles

Participating teachers agree on their various roles in the meeting. There are two major roles, facilitator and reflector, which require fluency in the conversational moves the teachers have learned previously through professional development, including learning about discourse and deconstruction. Teachers can choose to be contributors, participants or observers, gradually easing into the roles of facilitator and reflector as they become more competent in the conversational moves necessary for those roles. The facilitator and reflector roles are pivotal. The facilitator is responsible for setting behavioural expectations, maintaining the structure and flow of the meeting and asking appropriate questions throughout. The reflector role requires competence in discursive reflection and deconstruction in order to identify and unpack the unhelpful and helpful ideas that are affecting relationships in the classroom. Participant teachers are encouraged to ask curious or deconstructive questions, as they see appropriate, using externalising language and avoiding totalising language throughout the meeting.

Setting up a circle

Before the meeting, one of the teachers rearranges the seats in the classroom into a circle format with help from students.

The actual meeting

Karakia and starter activity

The class meeting always begins with a reflection or a karakia (spiritual invocation said in Māori). The inclusion of this step is seen as showing respect for the meeting protocols of the indigenous people of the country, which are frequently observed during public meetings in New Zealand. The formal opening of the meeting is followed by a starter or mixer activity, discussed previously. The starter activity is designed to get students and teachers speaking to each other and getting to know more about the classroom community. Activities to get students to mix up their seating arrangements are used to encourage a supportive environment.

Introducing people and process

The meeting continues with participating teachers introducing themselves (if they are unknown to the class) and their roles in the meeting.

The facilitator explains (or reviews) the process and the rounds that will be followed. There is an explanation of the relevant key competencies and examples of what would constitute a display of such competence during the class meeting. For example, explaining the messages consciously and unconsciously sent with the body and the various power relationships that body language can call into being has been a distinguishing feature of the meetings, which provide a good opportunity to help students understand how their body language sends messages of respect (or not), as well as learning to read non-verbal cues (Frey & Davis Doyle, 2001; Marshall, 2001).

Giving the context
The facilitator or one of the teachers provides a rationale for the meeting. In the following example of a Year 10 class meeting, Ms Smith, the form teacher, addresses the class using externalising language and avoids blaming particular students like this:

> I have called this meeting for two reasons. First, I want to acknowledge how much better the class has been working since our last meeting a month ago. I and the other teachers have all noticed the help that you give to each other and the longer periods of on-task behaviour. However, during last week I noticed that learning had stopped being a priority and there was a general lack of interest to complete assignments. I have also found out, talking to some students, that several of you are finding the social environment uncomfortable, if not threatening. There seems to be a bit of meanness creeping into relationships. As you can see, all your subject teachers and your deans are here to find out what you think might be happening and how we could go back to the calm working atmosphere that we had a week or so ago and to stop things from deteriorating.

The four rounds
The facilitator then leads the discussion, structured into four rounds. She or he ensures that each and every student and teacher contributes to each round. With additional clarifying and deconstructive questions (asked by the reflector, the facilitator, participating teachers and sometimes students), there is not always time to complete all four rounds.

In those instances, remaining rounds will be covered in a subsequent meeting, usually the following day. This is not considered a problem as Māori meeting protocols require participants to devote as much time as it takes to resolve an issue. Clock time does not dictate what happens, but honouring every part of the process and the contributions of the participants does. The four rounds are an adaptation and simplification (given the number of participants) of a meeting format suggested by The Restorative Practices Development Team (2004). The rounds also loosely follow the process employed in narrative therapy. First the problem's influence on the class community is discussed, followed by the group's influence on the problem (Morgan, 2000).

Round one

In round one the issues affecting teaching and learning in the classroom are named and everyone's views on what the problems might be are listened to. Questions that might be asked include:

- What do *you* think are the issues/problems that need addressing in this classroom?
- What issues or problems undermine learning in this classroom?

Students are encouraged to speak in full sentences, and sentence starters are provided when students are new to the process or do not feel comfortable speaking in front of others (e.g. 'I think an issue that needs addressing is …' and 'I think the problem is …'). The students in Ms Smith's Year 10 class responded along the following lines:

> I think there is a general lack of respect in our class for both students and teachers.

> I think there is too much talking and distractions. When the teacher talks, some people talk over her and others lose focus and start talking, too. We get very little work done.

> There are people who are not interested in learning and they are consistently off-task and defiant. They make it difficult for those who want to learn.

> People bring their social dramas into the classroom and they tease and bully others.

Students also commented on teachers' practices:

> I find it difficult to listen when Mr Green talks too quietly.

> I lose interest when Ms Brown gets impatient and does not wait for us to complete the task.

Teachers also share their take on the problem when it is their turn to speak. When there are several teachers in the meeting, they sit at different points of the circle.

During the summarising of the major themes in the first round, deconstructive questions can be posed by the reflector or any of the teachers. The reflector's summary is meant to identify and expose some of those unarticulated but inferred ideas of schooling and relationship conduct that are likely to produce disruptive or unsupportive behaviours. In Ms Smith's class, different understandings of the leadership role of the teacher might be highlighted, along with what it might mean to be considerate towards others. Questions like these might be asked:

> Is it reasonable to expect that you can do whatever you like or talk when you are finished and others are not?

> How much waiting time would be fair? How would teachers know the difference between someone struggling and wasting time?

Such questions invite students to reflect on the effects of both student and teacher behaviours on others.

Round two

In round two the effects of the issue(s) are explored, with questions such as:

- What are the effects of the problems discussed on you, on others, or on learning?

Ms Smith's class identified the following effects that the occasional absence of learning behaviours brought about:

> We don't get any work done.

> People who want to learn do not get anywhere.

> It is hard for teachers to teach us and they get angry.

> The social dramas waste a lot of time. I don't want to do any group work,

because I am expected to get involved in the dramas and take sides.

You get attacked, if you don't get involved in the dramas.

Teachers might contribute along the following lines:

I am really disappointed when I prepare lots of interesting activities but get constantly interrupted when I try to explain them.

Round three

In round three, exceptions to the problem are sought (the alternative story) using questions like:

- Can you think of a time when these problems do not affect this class or when teaching and learning are going well?

In this round, useful information can be collected about the strategies and circumstances that are more conducive to teaching and learning. Further ideas can be identified that are worth problematising and critiquing. This is another phase of the class meeting in which deconstructive questions can be asked. Ms Smith's students thought that there were fewer disruptions and greater respect between people when:

There is a seating plan and I do not sit next to my friends.

We have practical lessons, when there is no theory.

I like the teacher or I like the subject.

The teacher makes the learning fun.

We all learn better when we are interested in a subject or we like the person who delivers the teaching. However, the idea that 'I will only collaborate with people I like or during subjects I prefer' is problematic for a learning community—for any community, for that matter. This idea privileges care for self and does not support the consideration of other people's interests. Deconstructive questions can invite reflection on such ideas and their implications for the various relationships within a classroom community.

Round four

In round four, participants are asked to make a commitment to something they believe would help address the problem and/or change the learning environment in positive ways. Both students and teachers are invited to answer the question:

- What are you personally prepared to do in order to improve relationships and/or learning in this classroom?

or:

- What do you think you need to commit to in order to improve relationships and/or learning in this classroom?

Both teachers and students commit to changing their practices, and these commitments are recorded in writing. Everyone writes down what they are prepared to do differently on a small card or Post-it. These commitments are collated on a large sheet of paper, which is usually laminated and displayed in the classroom. Such a public display of personal, signed commitments makes it easier to remind people of their promises if they forget to honour them. The meeting finishes with feedback, and participants—teachers and students alike—are invited to acknowledge individuals they thought showed competence in any areas of the key competencies. Ideas for future discussions and tasks for follow-up are recorded.

Teacher de-briefing after the meeting

Participating teachers allocate follow-up tasks, agree on the date of the next meeting, and decide what ideas (discourses) warrant further discussion, either with students or with colleagues. Collegial discussions of the various discourses exposed in class meetings often produce possible teacher responses for future conflict situations.

Results of investigations into these practices

Research on these practices is ongoing. The findings of studies done to date suggest the following.

Teachers reported an improved sense of wellbeing, though this was sometimes hard won. They felt that class meetings had made the job of teaching the class easier and felt more positive about their class, and that the meetings had made the class easier to manage. Students sometimes expressed reluctance about participating in the circles (also noted by Costello et al., 2010), but there was an improved learning environment and improved attitudes to learning for individual students (Kaveney & Drewery, 2011).

The restorative practices project referred to previously was voluntary, ran for 3 years, and involved around 20 teachers each year, with ongoing participation of those from previous years. In the early stages meetings were regularly video-recorded. Ethical permission was granted to study these video recordings from one class (Gray & Drewery, 2011). They showed significant shifts in behaviour of the class from the first meeting to the last. In particular, students expressed themselves better, were more considerate of others, and made longer and more appropriate contributions in the last meeting than they had done initially. These data suggest that students learned to manage themselves, to relate better to others, and to participate in their class community. In short, the classroom meetings helped students to learn—and demonstrate—key competencies

Commentary

While dysfunctional relationships—among students, or between students and teacher—precipitate the calling of a meeting, teachers do not set out to address problem behaviours as such. Students' behaviours are addressed in relation to their effects on the learning environment of the classroom. A study of students who have become disengaged with school (Gray, 2012) showed that positive relationships with peers and teachers helped them to continue their schooling. The climate of care and acceptance cultivated allowed these students to feel valued and encouraged. Teacher satisfaction has also been a focus from the outset. Many say that the approach has shown them how to relate better with students, which, in turn, affects their teaching.

We believe in the power of ideas to change lives. The results so far suggest it is worth pursuing the examination of the power of the dominating discourses that affect learning culture. Finally, a word about the effort involved. The ideas presented here may seem sophisticated, but teachers grasped them readily and took them up enthusiastically once they understood how easily they could change their ways of speaking and how effective this was. Though it does take personal commitment to acknowledge the potentially destructive effects of 'power over' relationships by teachers, it does not cost much to speak differently.

Summary of main points in Chapter 6

- Students as well as teachers can learn to problematise ideas that are governing classroom relationships.
- Behaviour modification approaches tend to focus too much on individuals and produce only temporary change.

- Thinking involves stepping back from what one is doing and reflecting upon its meaning.
- A deconstructive class meeting, a particular form of circle conversations, can enable the necessary thinking to happen, which in turn can improve teacher–student relationships.
- The quality of teacher–student relationships has been shown to directly correlate with students' achievement levels.
- Circle conversations produce an assemblage that can equalise the existing power relationships in a meeting.
- Circle conversations can create an intra-active flow in which people become more open to being affected by each other.
- Critique amounts to thinking differently about the discourses that are governing classroom interactions.
- Critique is necessary in response to a crisis.
- Teachers are encouraged to *listen* not only *to* what students have to say about their conflicts but also to *listen for* discourses of learning.
- Teachers can strategically use deconstructive questioning at various points in the class meeting.
- 'Learning should be fun' is an example of a strongly held but unhelpful idea that might be problematised and critiqued.
- A binary opposite of such an idea can be found, such as that learning requires hard work and practice.
- A plurality of meanings might be found between the polarised binary opposites. For example, 'Practice can be hard work but can also be made enjoyable.'

Exercise

The particular form of deconstruction introduced in this chapter aims to open for consideration different discourses or ideas about the topic in order to unsettle the dominance of a given idea or practice. The easiest way to do this is to identify the binary or polarised opposite of the dominant idea that is described as the participants' preference and thus accepted as the truth. Then the search for different ideas can focus on different notions that can be created between the polar opposites, or in a different combination of their elements.

In the example we gave, learning is only thought to happen when it is fun. An alternative discourse that interrupts the power of the 'fun' idea could be about the importance of work or effort or practice or perseverance, and so on. After identifying the binary opposition of a given idea (for example, work versus fun), which is usually an idea that is suppressed and not considered useful by persons in conflict, it should be introduced into the conversation with a question.

Teachers should first practise identifying alternative discourses and then come up with questions that would invite the evaluation of the effects of either the dominant or oppressed or another idea or practice. In the chart below, the statements in the first column were identified by teachers as problematic discourses. The statements in the second column were identified as possible alternatives. The third column is for possible different discourses that are hidden by the binary opposition.

Try to turn the statements in the second and third columns into questions that would invite clarification of students' (and teachers') ethical positions and that would question their usual ways of knowing.

Table 1: Problematising dominant ideas

Dominant idea	Binary opposite	Another possible idea	Questions
It's not fun so I just switch off and start talking to people.	Learning new skills requires work and investment of practice or perseverance.	Practice can be made more enjoyable and satisfying by the way we go about it.	
Teachers talk too much and it's boring.	Teachers have to explain new material and they have to introduce new information. It cannot be done in 2 minutes.	Teachers might give those who understand more quickly time to practise, while those who need further explanations can receive these.	
Teachers need to use our language.	Learning about a new topic means learning new vocabulary.	New vocabulary can sometimes be linked with local language.	

Why do we have to do it over and over again?	You need about 50 repetitions to remember something.	Some students need more repetitions than others.	
We do not need to ask any questions because we understand everything straight away.	Initial understanding does not always mean you know how to do it until you have practised.	Asking questions may bring up new aspects of knowledge.	
If I like the teacher, I will do the work.	Learning does not benefit the teacher as much as it does you.	Perhaps you might like the teacher more, if you work to get him or her to like you.	
Teachers should listen to us first, instead of us listening to them.	Learning something new requires that you be willing to listen.	Teaching and learning require exchanges between teachers and students.	
He was mean to my friend, so I just punched him.	Punching someone is also mean.	There are ways to respond to mean behaviour other than punching.	

Create your own list of statements that you have heard on a recurring basis and that represent discourses about learning and relationship conduct in general. Come up with questions that would help evaluate the effects of these discourses or would introduce an alternative.

Questions for reflection

1. What are some discourses that govern classroom relationships in your classroom?
2. Can you render each of these discourses as a statement?
3. Are these discourses helpful for learning?
4. What is the polar opposite of each statement?
5. What other possibilities lie hidden between these polar opposites?

Chapter 7 A diffractive approach to thinking about professional practice and identity: "I knew I was a good teacher. I was teaching kids who were difficult to manage"

Introduction

'Diffraction' or diffractive analysis is a methodology drawn from qualitative research (Barad, 2007; Davies, 2014a, 2014b; Mazzei, 2014). In the previous two chapters, processes of problematisation were applied to support a collaborative examination—by teachers in discussion with colleagues, and with students—of various notions of learning and teaching that might place teachers and students in conflict. In this chapter we propose an approach to thinking about practice that we conceptualise using the term 'diffraction'. We are aware that it is a term not commonly used by teachers and educational researchers. Reflection, reflective practice and reflexivity are more frequently applied terms in relation to thinking about practice, which is regarded as an ethical obligation of effective teachers. Both students in initial teacher education as well as practising teachers are encouraged to think about, or reflect on, their practice as often as possible. Such thinking is widely regarded as the necessary pre-requisite for both practice improvement and ethical conduct. However, what the process of such thinking or reflection might involve or how it might be done often remain unspecified.

We want to distinguish the particular approach to thinking about professional practice and identity described in this chapter from approaches that identify other possibilities; for example, an approach that addresses 'what could be done differently', by focusing solely on 'what works and what doesn't work'. Within the approach that we distinguish by calling it diffraction or a diffractive approach alternative possibilities, or 'what could be done differently', are opened up through an analysis of complex interference patterns or intra-actions (Barad, 2007) between policies, individual teachers' and their schools' practices, and the material, cultural and social forces and contexts in which those practices are embedded. In addition, the identification and analysis of interference patterns helps make visible how discursive forces, or the power of ideas that we referred to previously, might shape the quality of people's relationships. While other approaches to reflection might also touch on such interferences, we believe they do not deliberately set out to do so. Within a diffractive approach a variation from the status quo emerges, in which a critique of the status quo is accompanied by a deliberate move to highlight patterns of interferences between teachers' practices and wider institutional, social, material, cultural, political and economic forces.

The diffractive approach can be facilitated among colleagues through a particular form of listening, or 'the stance of curiosity' introduced earlier. Thinking in this way about professional practice can offer teachers possibilities for acting differently in stressful situations that make the job of teaching difficult, along with building communities of concern.

Establishing a climate of listening, and acting from the stance of not-knowing (as described in Chapter 3), is not only important with students. It provides opportunities for teachers to listen to their colleagues without requiring these same colleagues to account for themselves according to the listeners' pre-existing ideas (Butler, 2005). It can increase teachers' capacity to practise an ethics that foregrounds relationality and enables a performative politics of including and recognising difference (Teague, 2015). Teachers listening in specific ways to each other's practice and identity narratives can also start an intra-active flow, similar to the one that circle conversations facilitate. The space can be opened up for diffraction: a way of thinking about practice that exposes patterns of interference or "the entangled nature of differences that matter" (Barad, 2007, p. 36), showing at the same time "how values are integral to the nature of knowing and being" (p. 37).

This is in contrast to reflection, which more often than not can only repeatedly represent the status quo. When such thinking is enabled by colleagues offering a specific form of listening, teachers are more likely to reveal complex entanglements of systems, practices, identities, thoughts, feelings, relationships—the wider social and material contexts in which an individual teacher's life and practices are embedded and by which she or he might be affected and is affecting others — rather than only a narrow account of their dilemmas.

Such an approach can be particularly useful in response to situations where there is an impasse and teachers feel powerless to intervene. It can widen narratives by identifying interference patterns between national policy, schools' organisational systems, colleagues' actions and student responses to conflict in a particular school, systems of student and resource allocation to classes, teachers' and students' thoughts, feelings, behaviours and material environments, the discourses they draw on and the meanings they make of their experiences. Thinking about all these can help go beyond approaches that centralise, and subsequently blame, the autonomous individual. A more relational view of practice, identity and ethics becomes available.

"I am stressed because I have to be in three places today"

Hannah shared the following story with some trusted colleagues who were part of a group that attended professional learning sessions together. Her colleagues were able to listen without demanding that she provide answers they already knew and that she behave according to their suggestions. This, in turn, supported Hannah with thinking diffractively about her work. We will explain what we mean in more detail later.

Yes, I am stressed because I have to be in three places today. I'm in the class for half of the day, sharing the class with another teacher and, all of a sudden, we've got five new children with high, high behavioural needs and the balance has tipped. It was so hard to manage. On Tuesday at lunchtime, I've never had this in my whole teaching career, I was so, so angry. Angry because I was trying to manage the whole lot and some colleagues even said, 'I will take your class.' I said no, and my senior teacher came down to talk about it but you cannot talk about it like that. I was trying to have my lunch and I was trying to supervise three children. There were three children I ended up sending to the withdrawal room, and I think that is what made me angry.

I was trying to get the notices to go home in my lunch hour, plus supervise the kids inside, and my senior teacher came down to talk and the teacher came back in, the other teacher, and there's this conversation between the three of us and I'm trying to do my written work, plus supervise the kids for lunch, and have my own lunch. I was getting so cross. Well, I decided I wasn't going to talk back. I was not going to discuss the situation. I was basically trying to catch my breath and trying to go to the toilet. So I just said, 'Excuse me,' and walked out and came up here to have my lunch. I said to my colleague, 'I'm not happy,' and she said, 'You know, you've got release time tomorrow, so come and talk to me.' I said, 'No, I'm busy tomorrow, I've got my time committed and I need a day to think about it.'

In the afternoon when I got home, I thought about it, and I thought I'm managing three lots of children, I'm doing release time for other teachers and you know the children, when their teacher is out of the classroom, they are a bit more challenging and so I'm having to work with that, plus with my reading group children, and I'm trying to work behind the screen. [At the time of sharing her narrative Hannah was part of a professional development programme of changing teacher practices. The programme included colleagues observing each other's teaching from behind a screen and teachers videotaping their teaching for discussion.] I am struggling with a particular child. Instead of 20 minutes, I am giving him 40 minutes, trying to push it really hard, and it is not my fault that he is not making accelerated progress. There are many dimensions to why he is finding reading difficult.

So I go into this class where there are 13 high behaviour need children. And how do you reach that many children and give them all a bit of an affirmation? There is one kid there who just swears at the teacher and his mother has been called in and it is so hard. It is so hard on the other children and it is so hard on the teacher. So things were getting pretty hard for me. The next day I went and asked the senior teacher, 'Look, can I talk to you? I'm feeling quite stressed about my job.' I asked a colleague to support me in the meeting and I decided to have it after school and I wrote down what my day is like. The meeting went on for an hour and a half, and while the senior teacher listened, there were other things that were raised that perhaps shouldn't have been, but never mind. Really what she said was that I should take stress leave the following day. I thought that was fine, but I realised I was actually quite physically unwell. I had an awful cold. I decided to go to bed early and I was not really feeling well, so I went to the doctor and he said I have got bronchitis and I was put on antibiotics. The colleague [who had acted as support in the meeting] rang me and I thanked her for ringing, because I had the impression that she really cared.

I was actually not well enough to come back to school on the Monday or the Tuesday, so I rang my doctor and I did have the Monday and Tuesday off. On Wednesday, I came back to school and I did have the release day. The senior teacher came to me and said that she did not find the conversation between us easy, because other issues were raised, and, because I was an experienced teacher, I should be able to manage the children, no matter how difficult they were and how many of them there were. I should be able to manage and that I would have to take a difficult class for the rest of the year. But I would get release time every Wednesday, something that I should have had all year.

The situation has improved, because I am getting every Wednesday off. The thing is, I can understand from a senior manager's point of view, who is managing the relieving budget, but I know that, if you are determined to support your colleagues, you can take money from another budget and juggle things around. I have never told anyone in my 30 years of teaching that I am stressed because of the job. We have highs and lows in our profession and we have stressful times and other things. And I'm not the only one. I went to the health and safety person and I know, when somebody is stressed, it has to be recorded. I said, 'I am stressed because of the job and the workload and I want it recorded.' When I talked about it with my husband he said, 'Well, have I looked at all the possibilities? Is it me?' But I am the one who is in it, I know the way things are organised and I felt it. I know that I was not physically well.

I came back and I knew I was a good teacher. I knew I was teaching kids who were difficult to manage. I am an individual and sometimes I am going to have difficulties in my job and need support.

What can we make of Hannah's story of distress?

Hannah's story reveals a particular discourse of professionalism that seems to be supported by senior managers and is thus dominant in her school. Those who draw on this discourse, like Hannah's senior teacher, seem to be blind to and are unable to notice the stark contrast between the care teachers are expected to provide for a diverse range of children and the support teachers can expect for their own wellbeing. It seems to be considered normal and accepted practice in Hannah's school for a teacher to be doing several things at the same time, even during their lunch hour, when they might need to care for their own bodies. Her senior teacher's arrival during lunchtime to talk about the difficulties there might be in her class positioned Hannah as a teacher who was thought to be able to manage indefinitely without responding to her own body's needs.

Shacklock (1998) highlighted how the ethic of care has long been a part of teachers' vision of professionalism, which goes beyond simply looking after children and includes "a moral commitment to teaching". He claimed that teachers' day-to-day enactment of care and the actual practices that teachers understand as care and include in a good teacher's practice repertoire could be traced in teachers' narratives of their work. These same narratives might also show the ideological influences that have an impact on teachers. Shacklock demonstrated through teachers' work narratives that the ethic of care can contribute to the intensification of teachers' work, compelling them to do more and more and to generate a desire to "care beyond the norm". He also identified some of the paradoxical effects of a commitment to care. When teachers considered caring to be a significant part of their work, they also became vulnerable to feelings of guilt and anxiety in situations where they believed they were unable to provide the level of care they deemed appropriate. More importantly, Shacklock also noted the potential "loss of an educational caring space for professional and social interaction where teachers can support each other in their work" (p. 197) as a result of the work intensification produced by providing more care.

Almost two decades later, Hannah's story confirms Shacklock's observations and conclusions. It also demonstrates, among other things, an approach to managing teachers within a school organisation that isolates them and holds them individually responsible when unrealistic expectations are placed on them and they cannot cope. The problem is located in teachers rather than in the workings of a system or in a management culture that fails to provide care for the carers. Hannah is expected to manage a higher-than-usual number of high-needs children because she is an experienced teacher. Her failure to meet unrealistic and unreasonable expectations is treated as a matter of competency rather than as a problem of inadequate support or of an unclear job description. Neither does the school seem to have clear systems of collegial support when teachers like Hannah are overwhelmed. Support seems to depend on the goodwill of individual teachers, and possibly on the quality of Hannah's relationships with her colleagues, as opposed to being offered after professional considerations of what might count as an excessive workload.

We have talked previously about the importance of recognition within available discourses and of the need to be recognised as belonging to normative categories by others. Being recognised as a normal or good person is equally as important for teachers as it is for students. However, Hannah's senior teacher implies that Hannah is an ineffective teacher because she is unable to manage a high number of difficult students as she should be able to do, based on her experience.

The senior teacher's response places Hannah in a category of teachers who are judged inadequate. The implication is that there is something wrong with Hannah's management style rather than with the systems of support offered. It is only Hannah's categorial difference from 'good' teachers that is commented on, while there is no consideration or examination of how the school's systems of student and release time allocation and senior managers' expectations of classroom teachers might produce Hannah's tiredness, stress and inability to cope. She is responded to as an autonomous individual, who is held solely responsible for her problems. She is not responded to relationally. We will come back to this point when we talk about relational ethics later.

First, let us insert here some of Turrini and Chicchi's (2013) conclusions about the transformation of traditional labour, which we think have some relevance for how *time* is managed and responded to in Hannah's school. Based on their research on theatre workers' experiences, these authors suggest that traditional labour is undergoing a transformation, which, in turn, leads to the development of a new relationship with time for the workers of the 21st century. This new relationship is mainly characterised by the loss of the measurability of one's work. Due to an increase in private contracts, people can choose to generate their product in informal spaces, outside workplaces also. Work thus becomes *general intellect*, which can spread into various spheres of people's lives or might even permeate their whole lives. This process not only increases the risk of self-exploitation, but it also contributes to the crumbling of the wage society, where labour is measured by time. The value of labour becomes relative; in other words, a socially *immeasurable activity*. One significant effect of such transformation of work is that it also "utilises subjectivity in new ways" (Turrini & Chicchi, 2013, p. 510). This means that people find it difficult to resist this process, as it also validates their preferred identities, ambitions and desires. Thus people almost collude in their own exploitation as they take up particular identities.

Although teachers' work is very different from theatre workers', as teachers are not privately contracted to do projects for their schools, there are some similarities between Hannah's situation and the one described by Turrini and Chicchi. We can say that the boundaries between Hannah's professional and personal activities have become blurred and leaky. Her professional tasks permeate the time available for her to attend to her personal needs. She continues to work during the interval when she would be entitled to attend to her own body's needs. She finds it hard to resist the demand on her time, as all the activities that she has to perform during her lunch hour also validate her preferred identity as a caring and committed teacher. Thus her subjectivity, and her desire to be recognised as a good teacher, are utilised in exploiting her. Her time becomes immeasurable by making what counts as professional and private time indistinguishable.

Analysis

Discourse: lines of force

The discursive turn in the social sciences has made "the constitutive force of discourse in the lives of subjects" evident over the last three decades (Davies et al., 2002, p. 291). For those of us who accept the premise that the subject is discursively produced, the challenge no longer lies in recognising that discourses "gift us with our existence" and shape "our desires, our beliefs in what is right—the things we are prepared to die for" (Davies, 2005, p. 2). Rather, it is about how to make sense of and how to manage the "ongoing inscriptive process" (Davies et al., 2002) of our subjectification. The constant state of flux that we are placed in, while we take up our identities from multiple discourses, provides a further challenge as we can no longer constitute ourselves within a secure, stable, singular identity narrative, familiar to us from liberal-humanist theorising.

While discourses gift us with our existence and make us depend on them for our identities, they also have the capacity to insert themselves into our consciousness without us noticing, thus "colonising our soul" (Davies, 2005, p. 2). Further, the colonising force of discourses works on persons in hidden, rather than obvious, ways. It is, therefore, difficult to make those forces visible and revisable. Using as an example Nelson Mandela's account of his own fear when he realises that the pilot of the plane he is about to board is black, Davies (2005) demonstrates the actual moment when Mandela recognises his soul being colonised by an idea that is contrary to his values. He is able to catch himself taking up the terms of the discourse of racism and that recognition produces a shift in his consciousness. Instead of allowing racist ideas to seep into his consciousness, he inserts his critique of the same ideas into his thinking.

However, the kind of resistance Mandela is able to put up might be more difficult than it seems. The task of becoming somebody involves us in taking up the thoughts and practices from the identities we are offered as recognisable categories and folding our experiences into such molds. Such taking ourselves up according to the terms of socially accepted or dominant discourses by behaving in ways they prescribe can afford us an existence as a 'normal' subject. Therefore, constituting ourselves this way can be more pleasurable than taking ourselves up according to the terms of marginalised discourses, because we are also rewarded with recognition as an acceptable person. The pleasures of such recognition can, however, make it harder for us to notice when discourses work against our best intentions. That is why we can also "find ourselves controlled by a discourse that runs against conscience and stifles consciousness" (Davies, 2005, p. 2). This was what Mandela described. In other words, while discourses can validate our preferred values and moral positions, with a simultaneous act of force they can also insert into our consciousness ideas that might force us to act contrary to our values or that are incongruent with our moral position.

Constituting her identity as a committed, conscientious and caring teacher initially makes it impossible for Hannah to admit the stress-producing effects of the discourse of professionalism that compels her to care beyond the call of duty and to fit more than she can manage into a day's work. This discourse manages to seep into her consciousness when she first tries simultaneously to do multiple tasks, giving up her lunchtime to supervise children and to organise the notices for home. However, her embodied responses—her intensive feelings of resistance and distress—signal to her that there is something wrong. The way the force of this discourse of professionalism works on her body thus helps her to recognise her 'caught-upness' in it. Like Mandela, she is able to shift her consciousness and she is able to resist her time and her energy being exploited in this way. She leaves her classroom and goes to have lunch, also refusing to have a discussion during lunchtime about professional issues with her senior colleague.

When she later retells these events to her trusted colleagues, who listen without trying to intervene in her narrative, in her retelling she repeatedly refuses to accept the position of incompetent teacher. On the contrary, she cites herself as a good teacher and her students' intensive behaviour needs as reasonable explanations for her difficulties: "I knew I was a good teacher. I knew I was teaching kids who were difficult to manage." She also rejects her husband's suggestion that the problem might be located in her. Instead, she locates the problem in the system by pointing to the disproportionate allocation of high-needs children to one class, and emphasises the necessity of increased support when teachers are overwhelmed. She normalises the difficulties that individual teachers might have as opposed to accepting them as a sign of ineffectiveness. She offers a solution for supporting overwhelmed teachers by way of reorganising the relieving budget.

Modes of engaging with lines of force: an ontological and political matter

If we accept that discourses work as lines of force that can shape practices and identities, then it matters how we engage with the force of discourses. Ransom (1997) suggests that the construction of ourselves as a person can either "be dominated by unacknowledged forces, in which case one's freedom is co-opted by external forces for external ends", or we can actively take charge of our subjectification if we are able "to intervene in and participate in determining the construction of one's [our] subjectivity" (p. 175). So we can say that it is our mode of engagement with the force of discourses that can make a difference for our lives. If we let the force of discourse "seep into our consciousness" without challenging or critiquing it, then we cannot be in charge of our subjectification. Our possibilities will be shaped by external forces, and the practices that we engage in will be dictated from the outside. However, we can also rupture the lines of force by inserting a critical consciousness. In this case, we will be in larger measure the authors of our own destiny; in other words, we can have a say in the development of our practices and identity. Our mode of engagement with discourses will thus determine what kind of a person we are able to become and what kind of identity we can take up.

Foucault (2000a, 2000b) calls people's different modes of engaging with the force of discourse "technologies of the self". He also offers some guidance on what kind of engagement or technology can weaken or rupture the force of discourses and support us with authoring our identities, just as Mandela and Hannah were able to do. First, we can recognise the presence of discursive forces when a concept or practice loses its familiarity. Foucault puts it this way:

> Actually, for a domain of action, a behaviour, to enter the field of thought, it is necessary for a certain number of factors to have made it uncertain, to have made it lose its familiarity, or to have provoked a certain number of difficulties around it. (p. 117)

We can say that, for Hannah, it was her commitment to her work and her care for the children that 'lost their familiarity' and became something different from how she used to experience them beforehand. Her work ceased to be the kind of pleasurable activity that it had used to be. It became instead burdensome and impossible to perform. For the first time in her teaching career she experienced herself as stressed about her job. Ordinary tasks, such as supervising children during lunchtime or sending notices home, turned into a struggle and became difficult to complete. Noticing her own resistance to this struggle also helped Hannah to realise how different her job had become from what it had used to be in the past. This recognition helped her to evaluate her changed circumstances and to critique the demands placed on her.

Out of fear Hannah could have continued to suffer quietly without challenging her senior manager. She could have accepted uncritically that this is how things are meant to be. She could also have internalised her senior teacher's implication of her incompetence by feeling guilty and doubting her skills as a teacher. She could have sought participation in further professional development in order to improve her classroom management skills. She could have put herself on a path of constant self-improvement, yet never have found herself good enough. And so on. Had she chosen this path, she would have practised what Foucault called a truth technology of the self, which he also considered to be characteristic of Christian and Western traditions of self-care.

A truth technology, Foucault (2000a, 2000b) claimed, is a technology of submission and obedience to rules, truths and to a master, rather than freedom and autonomy. Penitence, or disclosing one's sins to one's master and renouncing the self or its previous form, is the most significant practice of this technology. A 'sinner', or a person who has failed to behave according to the rules, has to renounce his or her previous self in order to transform it and to constitute it in new forms. What is required is the refusal of the past self rather than its acceptance. Obedience to a master, and sacrificing one's own will, are more highly valued than autonomy within this technology, while regimes of truth are not examined and reflected on either. Rather, they are used as the basis of coercive practice to support the self-regulation and control of persons. Had Hannah stayed in the classroom with her senior manager, after overcoming her initial resistance to and anger about the senior teacher wanting to have a professional discussion during lunchtime, she would have demonstrated the kind of obedience Foucault talks about. She would have accepted as the truth what her senior teacher (her 'master') suggested, as opposed to asserting her own views. She would not have questioned the regimes of truth, according to which it was fine to erase self-care from her lunchtime 'to do list'.

Ball (2006) suggests that teachers' work, and educational contexts in general, are increasingly characterised by an emphasis on practice improvement, assessment and accountability. The demands this places on teachers increase their ontological insecurity. In other words, they find it hard to claim a secure identity for themselves. Instead, they might often be overcome with self-doubt and guilt and subsequently intensify and internalise self-surveillance, constantly checking whether or not they are good enough. It is, therefore, imperative, according to Ball, that teachers have tools of critique that help them to understand and stay in control of their own identity work. However, in an educational climate where ongoing practice improvement and practice change are privileged, it might be difficult for teachers to devote equal attention to understanding their subjectification. It also requires a different process from examining practice through lenses of what works, in order to constantly improve it. A much messier process of problematising practice—or going beyond given regimes of truth, as opposed to accepting them—might be what is called for.

Foucault (2000a, 2000b) offers an alternative to the previously described truth technology. He calls it the technology of the care of the self, which was a Stoic practice in ancient Greece and Rome. In distinguishing it from Christian and Western truth technologies, Foucault termed the Stoics' rules of personal and social conduct 'the art of life'. For the Stoics, care for the self (sometimes called concern for the self) was associated with morality and ethics. To exercise self-care was a moral obligation, a political responsibility and a permanent duty of one's life. Self-care involved various activities, or, as Foucault says, "a network of obligations and services to the soul" (p. 232), including letter-writing and being reflective. Although care for the self was ontologically and ethically prior to caring for others, it did not mean neglecting care for others. On the contrary: it had to be done without an expense to others.

Care for the self was also associated with autonomy and freedom. Individuals were required to decide what they considered an acceptable form of existence, as opposed to others deciding it for them. So in contrast to individuals submitting themselves to others' notions of what they might become, through obedience to a master or to norms, as in the previously described truth technologies, the Greek notion of self-care valued autonomy and individuals being in charge of their subjectification. We can say that they preferred a mode of engagement with the lines of force in discourses that made it possible to rupture those lines of force, when considered necessary, and intervene in their own subjectification, instead of letting it be dictated by others.

We think it matters, both ontologically and politically, how teachers engage with discursive forces and whether they intervene in their work or not. What is at stake ontologically is who is able to define the kind of teacher identities that teachers can take up: teachers or others outside the teaching profession? It matters whether teachers can constitute themselves as agentive subjects, who can articulate what is reasonable in their work, and how they can withstand the power of discourses that undermine their professional authority. It matters whether teachers, like Hannah, can insert their own consciousness rather than letting the force of a particular discourse dictate the practices they should engage in and the kind of person they should become. The way teachers constitute their professional identities is also a political matter. If the members of the teaching profession only use truth technologies for self-care, then their professional autonomy and self-regulation might be at stake.

It is clear from the above that truth technologies are more likely to confirm the status quo than technologies of the care of the self. The kind of problematisation and critique that we have introduced so far, we believe, can not only be useful when there is a conflict between teachers and students or students and students, and when notions of teaching and learning have to be unpacked in order to reveal their harmful effects on relationships in the classroom. These processes have a place in supporting individual teachers to constitute their professional identities and practices, with support from colleagues. After all, a teacher feeling distressed or powerless to intervene in the circumstances that shape their work can be considered a crisis, just like an ongoing classroom conflict.

There are many teachers who might frequently have similar experiences to Hannah's. It is probably not difficult to find teachers who, at times, feel insecure about their own professional identity and practice and who are also stressed about the demands of their jobs. For those teachers it is important that they be able to define the kind of identities they want to take up, and to question the regimes of truth that might force them to act contrary to their values or to take on more than they can manage. This requires an awareness of the discourses through which they are constituted and constitute themselves, so that they can "find the lines of fault in and fracture those discourses. And then, in those spaces of fracture, speak new discourses, new subject positions, into existence" (Davies, 2005, p. 1).

So how could teachers facilitate a mode of engagement with the force of discourses that would also support going beyond a repetitious validation of the status quo? Next we will expand on our earlier arguments in support of the stance of not-knowing that we introduced previously. We claim that the significance of such a stance lies in supporting teachers to decide what they consider to be an acceptable form of existence. We shall also highlight the differences in the quality of thinking about practice that such listening can produce, in contrast to thinking that focuses on practice improvement only.

Listening: suspending the demand for a coherent narrative

We have argued before that listening from the stance of not-knowing helps generate new meanings and can be more productive in conflict situations than listening that seeks information, or the already known. Remember Andrew, the dean, and his conversations with John and Anna, which proved his preconceived ideas about John's and Anna's relationship wrong? We also talked about listening *for* discourses when we introduced the concept of re-positioning. You might remember how Cath, the principal of a school for students with challenging behaviours, was able to hear, in Robert's misbehaviour, his protest against injustice and how she then offered him a position outside a discourse of schooling as usual, where he could get out of a conflict situation with dignity (Laws & Davies, 2000). In both instances these teachers were open to accepting other ideas besides their own. They were willing to tolerate the temporary uncertainty required to get through the situation. Laura Teague (2015) provides further arguments, based on Judith Butler's (2005) work, for the usefulness of suspending our desire to know, while listening to students. She proposes that such listening supports a relational ethics and performative politics of inclusion, because it is more likely to offer recognition to students as a 'normal' subject within available educational discourses. We briefly summarise her examples between teachers and students before showing the relevance of her points for supporting stressed teachers.

Teague also cites our earlier re-positioning example of Cath, who offered a position outside usual school discourses to Robert when he was shouting obscenities on the roof of the school. Robert accepted Cath's offer of the position of protester against injustice and the conflict situation was resolved. However, with another example Teague also demonstrates that a teacher's good intentions to introduce a different discourse might not always be met with the same acceptance that Robert offered. Instead of opening an escape route from a difficult situation, the alternative position introduced can reinforce existing power relationships. When Teague's student, Thomas, aged 8, stated that only boys have muscles and girls have boobies, the teaching assistant responded to him by flexing her muscles and claiming that women can have strong muscles also. Although Thomas reluctantly answered,

'No,' when asked if it was true that only boys had muscles, he then quickly exited the conversation and ran away.

Teague argued that the discourse offered as an alternative was familiar only to the teachers, but not to Thomas. The adults insisted that "he recognise an identity that does not make sense to him" (2015, p. 401). Thus the offer privileged the teachers' knowing, while it also disregarded the power relationships among the children in the school. The teacher's responses did not take into account that Thomas had already been positioned as inferior in the social hierarchy established by the school's dominant discourses of masculinity. He, therefore, depended on those discourses for recognition. Accepting an alternative could have put him in danger and could have made him less recognised among his peers. Instead of fully accepting a yet unfamiliar discourse to him about women, he ran away, which Teague suggested was a justified response, both according to the systems of recognition and validation available to him and according to the positions he occupied in the school hierarchy.

This example demonstrates that offering alternatives on the listener's terms can be dangerous. In Thomas's case, the danger was produced by the teachers ignoring both his marginalised position within the school's dominant discourses and the "institutional power conferred on us [teachers] via the same discourses" (p. 401).

In Teague's other example, Dillon, aged 6, who had diabetes and had to eat at certain times, refused to eat his sandwich at the designated time. His teacher aide tried to convince him otherwise, as there was a health risk involved. If Dillon did not eat, he could lose consciousness. Dillon still refused. His teacher aide claimed that she could not help him unless he helped her. His teacher tried another approach and asked a question about his sandwich, wanting to know if there was anything wrong with it. She expected an answer that would help her understand how the sandwich might be the source of the problem. However, instead of providing an answer about his sandwich, Dillon kept talking about what had upset him in the previous lesson. He claimed that he could not log out of a program. His narrative did not make any sense to his teacher, because she knew that the program Dillon was talking about did not have a password. However, she temporarily gave up trying to force Dillon to eat and she listened. Her willingness to take a risk and listen to Dillon's seemingly incoherent story invited collaboration from him.

Teague claims that initially both the teacher aide and the teacher assumed that they knew themselves and Dillon, including what might have been the source of his problem. Yet demanding that he account for the problem on their terms invited more resistance, rather than collaboration, from him. It was only when his teacher was able to "suspend the desire for immediate and complete knowledge" (p. 407) and stopped asking for an explanation that Dillon complied. It was the teacher's willingness to tolerate not knowing and, more importantly, Dillon's incoherence, that created a space for Dillon to exist within the system of the school without being excluded. Dillon did not have to take up a subject position that was chosen for him by his teacher from among the available discourses, which was the case for Robert in our previous example of re-positioning. Rather, he was allowed to stay incoherent to his teacher, at least temporarily, which opened the space for a relational politics that allowed a more meaningful relationship to develop between teacher and student.

Drawing on Judith Butler's work, Teague proposes that if listening is only offered in order to require the other to account for themselves on the listener's terms and to answer the listener's questions, it constitutes a violent ethics. A relational ethics requires us to acknowledge "the unknowability of ourselves and each other" and "to understand incoherence, that which confuses, disrupts and dispossesses us of our narratives" (Butler, 2005, p. 64). Teague's interaction with Dillon is an example of an enactment of such relational ethics. Although she finds "[t]he suspension of the desire to know and to remain completely coherent" (p. 407) difficult, because it also undermined her recognisability as a teacher, not insisting that Dillon present a rational narrative to her "allows Dillon to re-enter a place of recognisability" (2015, p. 407) within the school.

For teachers like Hannah, recognition as a good teacher might be just as important as recognition as a good student is for Dillon. Yet we have witnessed many times that the kind of distress narratives Hannah related might, more often than not, be found incoherent and termed 'moaning' by colleagues. More often than not such narratives also fail to garner sympathy and support. The listeners to such stories find the detailed listing of events that cause stress and the frequent flitting from one event to another and back, as opposed to observing a 'rational' timeline, difficult to respond to. It does not help that stressed teachers often seem to repeatedly retell the same story over and over again. The receiving audience might find this a waste of time at best, or seriously annoying at worst. Hannah noted that she had also repeatedly told her story to various colleagues but was only able to list the events that caused her stress. In those tellings she was not able to articulate what she thought was reasonable to expect of a teacher, and neither was she able to firmly claim a professional identity position for herself, or comment on the systems of the school, as she was able to do when she was listened to by colleagues in her professional development peer group.

We think the difference in the various tellings was produced by the quality of the listening that was offered to Hannah. When Hannah had a meeting with her senior teacher and the health and safety person, she was only able to identify the events that contributed to her tiredness and stress. She was only offered positions that her listeners chose for her. According to her senior teacher, she was an experienced teacher who should have been able to manage any number of difficult children. Her stress and tiredness therefore contradicted this knowledge about her and were considered incoherent and irrational by her manager. The senior teacher could not stay with her own confusion or allow the narrative she knew about Hannah to be disrupted by a different story. Neither could Hannah account for herself within the senior teacher's narrative. The articulation of her preferred identity, the alternative possibilities for action and the questioning of the regime of truth the senior teacher drew on were also missing from the telling that she performed in the presence of her senior teacher. Yet she was able to put these forward in the presence of her peers.

Hannah's professional development peers were able to tolerate the unknown and they did not insist that she explain herself on their terms. They suspended their desire for complete coherence and knowledge of her. This, in turn, supported Hannah to be in charge of her own subjectification. She was able to reject what she thought was an unreasonable expectation and she was able to assign herself the identity of a good teacher. In addition, she was also able to claim the inadequacy of the school's support systems, as opposed to accepting negative judgements of her own competence. The relational ethics practised by her professional development peers supported Hannah to intervene actively in the lines of force and discourses that were constituting her own identity. She was able to go beyond reflecting on her own practice according to what works and what does not. She could think about her professional practice and identity diffractively. We conclude this chapter with a brief outline of the differences between using a 'what works' framework and a diffractive approach to thinking about practice and identity.

Diffraction versus reflection or reflexivity

Davies (2014a), in explaining what is involved in diffraction or diffractive thinking as it relates to qualitative research, distinguishes diffraction from reflection or reflexivity, which she says "seeks to *represent* what is already there" (p. 2). However, it is impossible to pin down or repeatedly represent something as it is. Barad's (2007) term 'diffraction', which is based on physics experiments with patterns of light, is, therefore, more useful, because it describes the ongoing production of something rather than its representation as already there. Diffraction does not simply fix things as they are. Neither does it document difference, as reflection would do. Diffraction is a process whereby a difference is made. It helps "illuminate differences as they emerge" and allows us to see "how different differences get made, what gets excluded and how these exclusions matter" (Barad, 2007, p. 30). More importantly, diffraction helps "track the interference patterns, and discover from them the ongoing diffractive processes through which the world creates itself" (Davies, 2014a, p. 3). So what would diffractive thinking about practice and identity look like and how would it differ from thinking about practice within a 'what works' framework?

Through her colleague's ability to offer a not-knowing stance, Hannah is supported to think diffractively and critically about her practice. Instead of repeatedly retelling her situation as it is and trying to represent the status quo by listing the causes of her stress and tiredness, the telling she performs in the presence of supportive colleagues produces differences in her professional practice. She rejects the practices she considers beyond the call of duty and accepts as legitimate her choice of self-care over school duties without guilt. These differences emerge as she is talking about her work. She herself is becoming different during the process. She is able to justify taking time off school because she was sick. Although she still has some doubts about her choice, she is able to question her senior manager's insinuation that she is not competent. She questions the school's practices of how children are allocated to teachers and the kind of support that is provided to those who might have to look after more challenging children or children with specific learning needs.

A different identity position from the one she took up before also emerges in her telling. She is not willing to let others be in charge of the production of her identity and to accept and submit to the senior manager's 'truth' about herself—that she should manage. On the contrary, she cares for herself by validating as reasonable options her taking time off at lunchtime and then from work. She calls into question the demands placed on her as unreasonable and impossible to comply with. In short, during the telling in front of her trusted colleagues, Hannah makes a difference for herself.

Hannah also interferes in her own thinking as usual, because she is able to identify and illuminate some of the interference patterns of her school's practices. This is where she is able to go beyond simply describing and evaluating her situation as it is and offering ideas about what she could do differently. Like the patterns of light that Barad describes, her thinking bounces in multiple directions. She establishes a connection between how the number of children with special needs in a class and the insufficient teacher aide and systemic support affect her ability to cope and stay on top of things. She articulates how she is affected by the school's systems, but she also affects those systems after returning from sick leave. She is offered more support from the principal and some regular time off, something she would have been entitled to receive earlier. Thus the encounter with her senior manager, where she leaves the conversation and the classroom, starts a series of movements. Hannah changes her own practice, her perception of her own identity, but also the meanings she makes of the school's practices, which, in turn, contributes to changes in the school's practices of support. Hannah is able to go beyond incessantly repeating—representing—what she is unhappy with. Diffractive thinking about her practice actively changes the way things are. Both Hannah's and the school's practices become different and further possibilities for different action are opened up.

We believe that if colleagues can listen to each other, suspending their demand for coherence and knowing the other person, a similar kind of intra-active flow can be started to that which circle conversations can achieve. Subsequently, teachers talking about their practice and identity to an audience that accepts their distress narratives without questioning them, or expecting them to answer according to the listeners' knowledge, can support a form of critique that goes beyond the kind of thinking about practice and identity that only involves the repetition of what is already known. Instead of the kind of thinking that exclusively focuses on practice improvement, which is so commonly asked of teachers, diffractive thinking about practice can be opened up. Such thinking goes beyond considering an individual teacher's practices by revealing at the same time some of the complex entanglements of organisational systems, institutional practices, patterns of relationships and the tensions between preferred and mandated identities. This in turn can enable teachers to go beyond their individual problems and to intervene in the development of their practice and identity by interrupting the force of discourses that shape school systems.

Summary of main points in Chapter 7

- Some approaches to thinking about practice only represent what already is, and do not consider challenges to the status quo.
- Diffraction disentangles discourses and lines of force and allows for systemic and relational thinking.
- Within a discourse, a teacher is recognisable as a 'normal teacher'.
- Discourses of care can render teachers' relationships with their work immeasurable.
- The challenge is to analyse how subjective experience is inscribed in discourse.
- It is possible to catch the moment when a discourse colonises our souls and resist the line of force that it creates.
- Foucault called our modes of engagement with the work that discourses do 'technologies of the self'.

- A 'truth technology' requires us to submit and be obedient to the rules or truths.
- The discourse of continuous improvement and accountability is based on a truth technology.
- A 'care of the self' technology allows teachers the freedom to intervene in their own subjectification and find the lines of force that are worthy of resisting in regimes of truth.
- Listening from a not-knowing stance allows others to engage in the care of the self.
- Open listening allows diffraction to occur and makes systemic interferences visible.

Exercise

This is an exercise for a small group of teachers to engage in a conversation. Share among yourselves examples of interactions you have had in the school in which you have felt that your status as a good teacher has been questioned. Try to listen to each other's experience of these stories without rushing to understand, and preserve the stance of not-knowing as long as possible. With each story, tease out the lines of force at work in the situation. In other words, practise the art of diffraction. Help each other identify the ways in which each teacher might intervene in the construction of his or her professional self.

Figure 6: Diffraction

Diffraction				
Line of force	Discourse	Line of force	Discourse	Line of force

Mode of engagement

Truth Technology   Care of the Self

Colonising the soul   Intervening in one's subjectification
Obedience   Systems change is possible

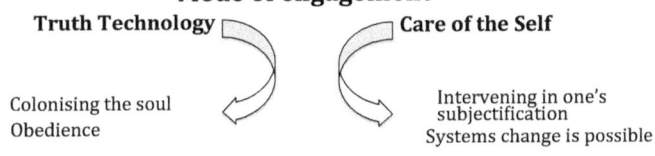

Questions for reflection

1. How have you noticed a 'truth technology' operating in your context of work?
2. Can you think of examples of when you have only been listened to within a colonising discourse?
3. What is it like to listen to a colleague from a not-knowing stance?
4. How might a 'care of the self' mode of engagement with one's professional development allow diffraction to occur?
5. What are some examples of the systemic or relational lines of force in a school that can interfere with the care of the self?
6. How might a teacher intervene to prevent these lines of force from dominating?

Chapter 8 Introducing the relationship-centred approach to teachers

Introduction

The relationship-centred approach outlined in this book includes both a theoretical framework for conceptualising principles of respect and participation, and conversational moves and processes that implement those principles in practice. We believe that this approach can also support teachers to uphold restorative principles, because it calls for taking a collaborative rather than an authoritarian stance. The conversational moves adapted from narrative therapy can be usefully incorporated into teachers' existing interactional repertoire without interrupting the flow of a lesson, while upholding restorative principles of respect and tolerance for differences. The same conversational strategies can also be used as part of more complex, multi-step processes, such as class meetings. Class meetings can be utilised by teachers who are willing to allocate more time not only to addressing relationship problems, but also to engaging students in conversations that aim to establish a classroom culture conducive to learning and teaching.

The emphasis of the relationship-centred approach is on respectful classroom interactions and prevention. The aim is to change teachers' ways of speaking and interacting through simultaneously teaching them both specific conversational moves and a theoretical framework that offers new perspectives on relationship problems. Therefore, it is important that within any professional learning dedicated to the introduction of the approach, equal time is allocated for skill practice and professional discussions, where theory is utilised to problematise, reconceptualise and change practice.

In what follows we outline the specific format of professional learning that was used to teach this approach to teachers in three schools. While it is possible to introduce this approach in many different ways, we believe that teachers learning to use a robust theoretical framework and being allowed sufficient time for thinking about their professional practice applying that framework can provide significant support for practice change and the development of teachers' professional identity.

A format of professional learning

It is well established in the professional learning literature that embedding new practices into school systems takes considerable time (Timperley, Wilson, Barrar, & Fung, 2007). This provides a challenge, because resources—especially budgets for funding teacher release during working time—can be scarce. The three schools that introduced this approach to their teachers all made it one of the major professional learning topics offered over the course of an academic year. They all provided release time for teachers to attend an introductory workshop and then regular, usually 3-weekly, focus group sessions with a facilitator. In each of the three schools, participation in this particular professional learning option was voluntary, as teachers could choose which of the two or three options on offer they would like to take up.

While the content of the professional learning and the format of delivery were almost identical in the three schools, three aspects of introducing the approach differed in one of the schools, which was a secondary school: the timeframe, the funding, and the relationship of the facilitator(s) with staff. We will call this school Midway High School for easy reference. The two other schools, one of which was a primary school, opted for a 1-year introduction. They both used their annual professional learning budget to provide release time for teachers, who volunteered for this training. These two schools employed an outside facilitator. However, Midway High School won an innovations grant from the Ministry of Education, which partly paid for teacher release. They also used two members of staff—one of the deputy principals and the head of guidance counselling—to deliver the professional learning, and they opted for a 3-year gradual introduction.

The take-up of both the conversational moves and the theoretical concepts was most successful in Midway High, with most participant teachers incorporating newly learnt skills into their interactional repertoire. This suggests that the 1-year timeframe the other two schools allocated to the approach is not enough to embed these practices into a school's system. In addition, having onsite facilitators allowed the teachers at Midway to draw on local expertise and support while learning the new practices. However, it is important to acknowledge that employing such a model can also be fraught with problems due to the power relationships and hierarchies that exist in a school. We will describe the 3-year gradual introduction model, but the pattern followed over 3 years could also be adapted to a shorter programme.

Midway High School offered training in the relationship-centred approach to a new volunteer group of about 20 teachers at the beginning of each of 3 consecutive years. Those trained in the previous year could continue their training, if they opted to do so, in the following year, in a more leadership and collegial support capacity. Each new group of teachers were first given 'the whole picture' during a 2-day introductory workshop, where the theoretical concepts and the specific conversational moves that we covered in the previous chapters were each introduced, demonstrated and practised.

Two additional professional learning sessions were timetabled in each school term for all participating teachers. These lasted for 2 hours each and provided regular and ongoing opportunities for practice, discussion and development of the concepts and the conversational strategies. Teachers could also share and discuss articles and resources on relationship practice during whole-school professional learning meetings, which were held 4-weekly and lasted for an hour after school. These meetings further supported the acquisition of skills and the understanding of theoretical concepts.

When training is run by outside consultants, which is a model most schools use, it can add considerable costs and thus undermine the feasibility of such an intensive model. Local expertise in Midway High School, and the flexible timetables of the counsellor and the deputy principal who ran the professional learning, made it possible for teachers to also receive daily in-class support, when requested. Teachers could practise their newly learnt ways of speaking with support from colleagues in class meetings, gradually easing into more independent facilitation. The retention rate in the 3rd year was over 40 teachers out of the approximately 60 who had attended the introductory workshops and focus group sessions for at least a year. Midway High has over 70 staff.

Not making the training in the relationship-centred approach compulsory, we think, invited less resistance from those teachers who did not agree with the theoretical ideas that are central to this approach. Teachers were able to better focus on new learning because the training sessions were held during working hours and not after school or during school holidays. They could regularly draw on on-site expertise and take advantage of the support the deputy principal and the counsellor could provide in their classrooms, which helped keep conversations about the relevance and various applications of the specific concepts and relationship practices of the approach alive on a daily basis. Teachers' feedback about their experiences of the ideas and practices thus contributed to the further development and fine tuning of the approach.

The critical role of thinking differently about practice

Most new relationship practices are introduced to teachers because of concerns about students who are either the recipients or perpetrators of bullying, or the targets of punitive disciplinary measures because of their disruptive behaviours. While changing student behaviours and creating classroom communities supportive of learning are expected outcomes, the relationship-centred approach focuses on teachers. One of its distinct objectives is to develop teachers' capacity to think about the ethics of their practices, along with changing their ways of speaking and being open to different others when they respond to stressful situations. We believe that having a framework that can help teachers think differently about practice can also improve teachers' wellbeing. Teachers are a significant human resource. They are entrusted with the task of modelling and teaching peaceful ways of relating to students.

Stressed teachers are less likely to have the mental and emotional capacity to do this.

The relationship-centred approach gives as much priority to reflecting and thinking differently about practice as it does to the use of specific conversational skills. In particular, a deconstructive approach to thinking about relationships is taught and encouraged as a framework for professional discussions. The same amount of time is devoted to developing an awareness of, and a capacity to recognise and name, discourses as to developing competence in the use of conversational skills. There are a number of arguments for not privileging practice over theory. Most teachers are very busy, so their desire to seek out practices that offer quick solutions to problems is understandable, especially when they struggle with constant disruptions every day. However, the pressure to establish order can easily entice a teacher into privileging technical solutions and formulas, without giving sufficient time to integrating them with the teacher's values and teaching philosophy. Theorists and proponents of professional learning and organisational change warn that solutions not integrated with the particular philosophies of individual teachers are less likely to be utilised—either to their full potential or long term (Senge et al., 2000). Regular reflection and discussion opportunities within professional learning can support identity development and the clarification of teachers' moral positions, which, in turn, can have an enhancing effect on wellbeing. Having time for collegial conversations about the relationship problems and dilemmas individual teachers face can support the collective identification of recurring patterns and similarities of experiences, which, in turn, might facilitate collaborative problem solving and open different possibilities for action.

Workshops and focus group meetings

The introductory workshop is an integral part of the training. This is where 'the whole picture', the main theoretical ideas (including the notions of discourse, power/knowledge, the productive power of language, categorisation and normalisation) and the recommended conversational moves (for example, externalising, questioning with genuine curiosity, re-positioning and deconstructive questioning) are introduced. However, the major sites for teachers' learning of this approach are the sessions that we have termed 'focus groups' for easy reference. These differ from what is meant by focus groups in qualitative research. These focus groups are professional learning sessions, during which a group of six to 10 teachers meet with the professional learning facilitator(s) for about 2 hours minimum, twice a term, during an academic year. The sessions are intentionally planned and structured to fulfil multiple functions. These functions include the demonstration and practice of the conversational and analytical skills taught, professional discussions informed by a process of problematisation and deconstruction, and peer supervision. Thus focus groups are designed to be a complex combination of professional practice and identity development.

The central role of deconstruction

One of the unique features of focus group sessions, in addition to skill practice, is the use of a deconstructive problematisation process, which informs and structures teachers' discussions about the concerns and dilemmas they encounter in their work. It involves the identification of discourses and relationship patterns that teachers engage in with students, and of recurring themes that emerge from teacher–student interactions and class meetings. When teachers reflect on the range of discourses that affect their relationships with students, colleagues and parents, they are also invited to clarify their own position and stance on those discourses. In other words, they engage in exploring their own beliefs and values about teaching, which can develop professional identities and ethics.

Deconstruction supports the expression of difference because it can uncover and bring forward previously hidden or unknown perspectives, concerns and agendas. It works against the repression of concepts and subjects, so it is necessary for critical opposition to inform different action (Banister, Burman, Parker, Taylor, & Tindall, 1994; Parker & Shotter, 1990). It provides space for articulating multiple meanings and different perspectives by fostering "new networks of understanding" (Larner, 1999, p. 42). It reveals not only those less obvious assumptions that maintain particular practices but also those hidden binaries, ideas and discourses that might be oppressed because they stand in opposition to dominant ideas (Bansel, Davies, Laws, & Linnell, 2009; Davies, 1994, 1996).

Deconstruction challenges power relations by destabilising and complicating positions of power, and by revealing who is privileged or oppressed by a discourse and what moral orders it might authorise (Larner, 1999). Deconstruction interrupts the idea that one pair of a binary is superior to the other (Davies, 1996). It helps in the search for alternative ways of constituting identities by recognising patterns that individuals are caught up in, thus helping them unsettle the discourses that position them in opposition to others (Bansel et al., 2009). Deconstruction "turns the gaze" on discourses (Davies, 1998) and reveals them as complicit in the production and reproduction of problems, instead of blaming individuals.

There is a body of literature that recommends a discursive turn in teachers' thinking about their practice and professional development. Its proponents suggest that discourse knowledge and deconstructive skills can strengthen teachers' professional authority and agency in standing up to market agendas and in refusing to uncritically accept reforms (Davies, 2003). Critiquing dominant discourses is important if teachers want to have "emancipatory authority" and be "transformative intellectuals" (Harrison, Clarke, Edwards, & Reeve, 2003; Hursh, 2003; Satterthwaite, Atkinson, & Gale, 2003; Slater, Fain, & Rossatto, 2002). Discourse knowledge is also considered to be the educational profession's safeguard against governmentality (Armstrong, 2005; Hook, 2003) or, in other words, against teachers being instruments of disciplinary power. Discourse knowledge can help identify which discourses might produce teacher–student conflicts and reveal how they might work to undermine teachers' professional authority and capacity to teach.

Deconstruction supports engagement with the ethics of practice. It can be a tool of political and responsible action (Larner, 1999; Parker & Shotter, 1990) that helps maintain public awareness of the ongoing concerns of a profession and contributes to changing the conditions that undermine it. It invites taking a stand on discourses and deciding which to accept or to reject. It interrupts usual ways of thinking about problems (Clough, 2002; St Pierre, 2002; 2004), and it supports "asking questions previously unasked and unthought" (Larner, 1999). It can facilitate the kind of critical consciousness and understanding of the ideological influences on a profession that the proponents of critical pedagogy advocate (Freire, 1970; Giroux, 2004; McLaren, Martin, Farahmandpur, & Jaramillo, 2004). Deconstruction is credited by some with no less than helping teachers to consider the purposes and nature of education and whether to keep thinking of education as a service for the common good (Armstrong, 2005; Biesta, 2004; hooks, 1994), with teachers being accountable to their profession and society. Deconstruction can serve as a strategy for maintaining ongoing attention and sensitivity to the social context of education. It can also be a tool for challenging those discourses, policies and practices that do not promote respectful teacher–student relationships.

Last, but not least, deconstruction can facilitate professional and public discussion and debate by providing new understandings and perspectives on issues (Banister et al., 1994; Denzin, 2005; Parker & Shotter, 1990; St Pierre, 2002). Deconstructive approaches are a useful method for studying complexity because they set out to uncover what is not so evident in conversations. They can show up some of the elements of complexity: the messiness, the chaos and the lack of order of the many contradictory discourses that contribute to relationship trouble (Mazzei, 2004; St Pierre, 2004). With this book, we provide new perspectives on teacher–student relationships and conflicts that might also help foster professional and public dialogue about the purposes of schooling.

Focus groups as support for identity and practice development

The specific format of focus group meetings that we propose for professional learning utilises so-called outsider-witness processes sometimes used in narrative supervision (White, 1999). It is a structured way of facilitating the telling of practices and experiences. Colleagues listen to these tellings from a not-knowing stance without interruption. They are encouraged to suspend both their demand for a coherent narrative and their expectation that their questions will all be answered. They will then retell the narratives they have heard by adding their own meanings. However, these retellings are not meant as impositions of the certainty and superiority of their knowledge, but rather as wonderings about different, not-yet-entertained possibilities and perspectives that emerge during the telling and retelling. Such a process can enrich both practice and identity. It can also change unhelpful meanings and practices that support blame, self-doubt and guilt and subsequently increase teachers' stress levels. Teachers can perform their professional identity in front of their colleagues, while examining how their practices might be congruent (or not) with their moral values. Teachers can thus practise newly learnt skills in a safe environment, while sharing practices and ideas with their colleagues.

Focus group meetings can also support the telling and retelling of preferred identity stories. They provide opportunities for teachers to articulate and share with colleagues those narratives of their practice, identity and life that they find significant. The responses they might receive from colleagues could also contribute to further developing and enriching those narratives. Storying life events, qualities and competencies that make up their preferred identity but that might be forgotten or doubted as a result of the pressures and problems of school life in itself can improve teachers' wellbeing.

What teachers have said

We include here feedback from teachers who not only participated in professional learning about the relationship-centred approach but applied the theoretical ideas and conversational moves in their teaching practice on a daily basis. Several teachers commented that speaking differently in the ways introduced in this book had a positive effect on their own mental health.

> There is a temptation to just fly off the handle, put those kids in their place and have my own way, because I can do it quite well. But I know that that is the least productive way to do it now. I learned this in the first course we went through, but that actually isn't the best for my own mental health, because you go away seething about it. If you have these more open and honest dialogues, even if you haven't gotten your own way, when you go away, you feel OK. You think that's all right then, that's just the way it is. And if an adult feels like that, who is supposedly rational, then it is so that children do, too. So I try to talk to these children, when I see them in the playground. I try to keep the dialogue going on, whether they are being naughty or not, and I think that is helping.

Committing to staying with and consciously setting out to repair difficult relationships has not only made it easier to deal with difficult students, but also helped a teacher get through a particularly difficult time in her job, when she even entertained the idea of resigning.

> I think it has helped with the more difficult relationships. I think that with the ordinary ones we were probably dealing with quite well, but then this very difficult relationship came crashing down, out of the blue. I wasn't expecting it, but this year there have been big changes [in the school]. It has been good for me personally and also professionally, to have that time and step aside and reflect ... and for me this has given me a way to think through it. I go over things and I won't resign. There is a way and it is not hopeless. I think that is quite important personally. Without it I don't think I'd still be here, I don't think I would have found a way through it.

Listening from a not-knowing stance was important for exploring different views and making people feel listened to. Teachers believed that being able to put forward one's own point of view could lead to the resolution of problems. In fact, a person's capacity to voice his/her views was more important than resolving problems. Curiosity was seen to provide an opening for the admission, sharing and validation of different views.

> If you don't talk about the situation, then you could just end up with little niggly things just hanging in there. Resolving would be hearing everybody's point of view, no matter if it's a teacher or child, everybody has their point of view on an issue and I think it's really important that you listen to it. If things are left there, they can linger there for years. Gosh, families sometimes have things that go on for years. Well, you can agree to disagree, but it's really important that you are listened to, especially when you are in a situation when someone has more power, it's important that you are listened to. Really being listened to is more significant than the resolution. So yes, I do think that you do need to listen to each other and be allowed to talk to each other. The overriding principles of listening and accepting there are different views and giving everyone the chance to voice their views ... I think it's helped with adult relationships and that people have got different points of views and to accept that they shouldn't be thinking what I think. It's also good for your personal life.

Teachers found it equally important to suspend normalising judgements of students and be willing to revise their interpretations. This helped to explore the students' version of events and to show interest in their views. It also helped a teacher's preparedness to look at alternatives.

> I could have told the student you are a truant, you are a slacker and here is a list of what teachers have given me as evidence of that and I know all of that stuff is happening but I need to find a way forward for him. For me, it is trying very hard not to assume that I know where they stand on an issue and what's happening. If I kept assuming that actually I don't know, then it is much easier for me to keep asking questions to give me something that might clue me into what to do next. If somebody is growling or yelling, whatever the interaction is, if I don't presume and I ask a question about what is happening and what are you feeling, I'm much more likely to get good information. So, in a classroom you need those methods of allowing a student to know that you listen and that you are actually prepared to look at a problem in another way. And if you delay the discussion until another point in time, the students are much more willing, because they know you are listening.

Through using different ways of interacting, these teachers created new possibilities in their relationships with students and colleagues. Their conversations opened, rather than closed down, options. The conversational strategies also positioned students and colleagues as participants and contributors, rather than as passive subjects who need others to decide what they have to do. Those teachers who consciously applied the skills could articulate what identities they wanted to take up and they could choose the practice that validated it. In addition, they consciously considered the effects of their interactions, staying connected to the ethics of their practices. We think that a relational ethics that supports a continuous awareness during conversations of one's ethical stance and its potential effects on others is preferable to a stance that is blind to the implications of the practices it enables.

This specific approach to relationship practice is one possible response to the daily relationship challenges that teachers and students encounter in diverse classrooms. It is important to note that both the content (the theory and the ways of speaking) and the delivery method (the design of the focus group process to incorporate deconstructive thinking, problematisation and outsider-witness practices) are integral to the approach and they work best when used together. The approach was found to reduce teachers' stress through improving their capacity to manage differences and the complexity of their work (Kecskemeti, 2011). Other findings so far have confirmed the enhancing of wellbeing for teachers of the class meeting process that builds on this approach (Kaveney & Drewery, 2011) along with its potential to develop students' key competencies (Gray & Drewery, 2011). A less measurable but possibly significant impact of the approach was articulated by a colleague, who said: "Whatever the situation might be with resourcing, these practices will continue at this school, as they are now part of our lives. We use them every day in both our professional and personal relationships."

Closing remarks

In the rush to develop higher standards in schools through installing national curricula and introducing more frequent and more rigorous testing, relationships in the classroom can easily be neglected. Yet teaching and learning are built on relationships. This book places such relationships front and centre.

The usual approaches to classroom relationships are either teacher centred or student centred. In this book we have proposed a third way: relationship-centred classrooms. The approach to classroom relationships we have outlined can be learned by teachers and by teachers in training. It is based on a robust theoretical foundation and it demands commitment from students and teachers rather than advocating either rigid authoritarian or soft feel-good solutions.

Drawing on the literature on restorative practices, it takes a restorative approach to addressing problems rather than relying on punishment. We argue that classroom relationships are foundational for learning and have shown how to work with a range of relationship challenges that threaten to derail learning. We have outlined an approach that calls for teachers to think in fresh ways and to pay careful attention to their interactions with students, colleagues and parents. It shows them how to change their ways of speaking and thinking about practice.

We invite teachers and students to look beyond individuals and to make the social forces and power relationships that are operating in their classrooms more readily available for discussion. We want them to collaboratively examine and challenge ideas that maintain and reproduce conflict. This is an ongoing project, which we think can develop key competencies and a relational, ethical approach to participating in communities. Our hope is that schools and teachers will find inspiration in these ideas and will join us in advancing this project.

References

Anderson, H., & Goolishian, H. (1992). The client is the expert: A not-knowing approach to therapy. In S. McNamee & K. S. Gergen (Eds.), *Therapy as social construction* (pp. 25–39). London, UK: Sage.

Annamma, S. A., Boelé, A. L., Moore, B. A., & Klingner, J. (2013). Challenging the ideology of normal in schools. *International Journal of Inclusive Education*, *17*(12), 1278–1294. doi: 10.1080/13603116.2013.802379

Armstrong, D. (2005). Reinventing "inclusion": New Labour and the cultural politics of special education. *Oxford Review of Education*, *31*(1), 135–151. doi: 10.1080/0305498042000337237

Arribas-Ayllon, M., & Walkerdine, V. (2008). Foucauldian discourse analysis. In C. Willig & W. Stainton-Rogers (Eds.), *The Sage handbook of qualitative research in psychology* (pp. 91–108). London, UK: Sage.

Ball, S. J. (2006). The teacher's soul and the terrors of performativity. In *Education policy and social class: The selected works of Stephen J. Ball* (pp. 143–157). Abingdon, UK: Routledge Taylor & Francis Group.

Banister, P., Burman, E., Parker, I., Taylor, M., & Tindall, C. (1994). *Qualitative methods in psychology: A research guide*. Buckingham, UK: Open University Press.

Bansel, P., Davies, B., Laws, C., & Linnell, S. (2009). Bullies, bullying and power in the context of schooling. *British Journal of Sociology of Education*, *30*(1), 59–69. doi: 10.1080/01425690802514391

Barad, K. (2003). Posthumanist performativity: Toward an understanding of how matter comes to matter. *Signs*, *28*(3), 801–831. doi: 10.1086/345321

Barad, K. (2007). *Meeting the universe halfway*. Durham, NC: Duke University Press.

Biddulph, S. (2008). *Raising boys: Why boys are different and how to help them become happy and well-balanced men*. Lane Cove, NSW: Finch Publishing.

Biesta, G. J. J. (2004). Education, accountability, and the ethical demand: Can the democratic potential of accountability be regained? *Educational Theory*, *54*(3), 233–251. doi: 10.1111/j.0013-2004.2004.00017.x

Bishop, R., & Berryman, M. (2006). *Culture speaks: Cultural relationships & classroom learning*. Wellington: Huia Publishers.

Bishop, R., Berryman, M., Cavanagh, T., & Teddy, L. (2007). *Te Kotahitanga phase 3: Whanaungatanga: Establishing culturally responsive pedagogy of relations in mainstream secondary school classrooms*. Wellington: Ministry of Education.

Bishop, R., Berryman, M., Tiakiwai, S., & Richardson, C. (2003). *The experiences of year 9 and 10 Maori students in mainstream classrooms*. Wellington: Ministry of Education.

Burr, V. (1995). *An introduction to social constructionism*. London, UK: Routledge.

Burr, V. (2003). *Social constructionism* (2nd ed.). London, UK: Routledge.

Butler, J. (1995). Contingent foundations: Feminism and the question of 'postmodernism'. In S. Benhabib, J. Butler, D. Cornell, & N. Fraser (Eds.), *Feminist contentions: A philosophical exchange* (pp. 35-57). New York, NY: Routledge.

Butler, J. (1997). *Excitable speech: A politics of the performative*. New York, NY: Routledge.

Butler, J. (2004a). *Precarious life: The powers of mourning and violence*. London, UK: Verso.

Butler, J. (2004b). What is critique?: An essay on Foucault's virtue (2000). In S. Salih & J. Butler (Eds.), *The Judith Butler reader* (pp. 302–322). Oxford, UK: Blackwell Publishing.

Butler, J. (2005). *Giving an account of oneself*. New York, NY: Fordham University Press.

Clough, P. (2002). *Narratives and fictions in educational research*. Buckingham, UK: Oxford University Press.

Costello, B., Wachtel, J., & Wachtel, T. (2010). *Restorative circles in schools: Building community and enhancing learning*. Bethlehem, PA: International Institute for Restorative Practices.

Davies, B. (1990). Agency as a form of discursive practice: A classroom scene observed. *British Journal of Sociology of Education, 11*(3), 341–362. doi: 10.1080/0142569900110306

Davies, B. (1991). The concept of agency. *Postmodern Critical Theorising, 30*, 42–53.

Davies, B. (1994). *Poststructuralist theory and classroom practice.* Geelong, VIC: Deakin University Press.

Davies, B. (1996). *Power/knowledge/desire: Changing school organisation and management practices.* Canberra, ACT: Department of Employment, Education, Training and Youth Affairs.

Davies, B. (1998). Psychology's subject: A commentary on the relativism/realism debate. In I. Parker (Ed.), *Social constructionism, discourse, and realism* (pp. 133–146). London, UK: Sage.

Davies, B. (2003). Death to critique and dissent?: The policies and practices of new managerialism and of 'evidence-based practice'. *Gender and Education, 15*(1), 91–103. doi: 10.1080/0954025032000042167

Davies, B. (2005). The (im)possibility of intellectual work in neoliberal regimes. *Discourse: Studies in the Cultural Politics of Education, 26*(1), 1–14. doi: 10.1080/01596300500039310

Davies, B. (2006). Subjectification: The relevance of Butler's analysis for education. *British Journal of Sociology of Education, 27*(4), 425–438.

Davies, B. (2008). Re-thinking 'behaviour' in terms of positioning and the ethics of responsibility. In A. M. Phelan & J. Sumsion (Eds.), *Critical readings in teacher education: Provoking absences* (pp. 173–186). Dordrecht, The Netherlands: Sense Publisher.

Davies, B. (2009). Difference and differenciation. In B. Davies & S. Gannon (Eds.), *Pedagogical encounters* (Vol. 33, pp. 17–30). New York, NY: Peter Lang.

Davies, B. (2011a). Bullies as guardians of the moral order or an ethic of truths. *Children & Society, 25,* 278–286. doi: 10.1111/j.1099-0860.2011.00380.x

Davies, B. (2011b). Open listening: Creative evolution in early childhood settings. *International Journal of Early Childhood, 43*(2), 119–132. doi: 10.1007/s13158-011-0030-1

Davies, B. (2013). Normalisation and emotions. In K. G. Nygren & S. Fahlgren (Eds.), *Mobilising gender research: Challenges and strategies* (pp. 21–30). Forum for Gender Studies: Mid Sweden University Working Papers 5. Sundsvall, Sweden: Mid Sweden University.

Davies, B. (2014a). *Listening to children: Being and becoming.* Oxfordshire, UK: Routledge.

Davies, B. (2014b). Reading anger in early childhood intra-actions: A diffractive analysis. *Qualitative Inquiry, 20*(6), 734–741. doi: 10.1177/10778004 1 4530256

Davies, B., Browne, J., Gannon, S., Hopkins, L., McCann, H., & Wihlborg, M. (2006). Constituting the feminist subject in poststructuralist discourse. *Feminism & Psychology, 16*(1), 87–103. doi:10.1177/0959-353506060825

Davies, B., De Schauwer, E., Claes, L., De Munck, K., Van de Putte, I., & Vertichele, M. (2013). Recognition and difference: A collective biography. *International Journal of Qualitative Studies in Education, 26*(6), 680–691. doi: 10.1080/09518398.2013.788757

Davies, B., Flemmen, A. B., Gannon, S., Laws, C., & Watson, B. (2002). Working on the ground: A collective biography of feminine subjectivities: Mapping the traces of power and knowledge. *Social Semiotics, 12*(3), 291–313.

Davies, B., & Gannon, S. (2012). Collective biography and the entangled enlivening of being. *International Review of Qualitative Research, 5*(4), 357–376. doi: 10.1525/irqr.2012.5.4.357

Davies, B., & Harré, R. (1990). Positioning: The discursive production of selves. *Journal for the Theory of Social Behaviour, 20*(1), 43–63. doi: 10.1111/j.1468-5914.1990.tb00174.x

Deleuze, G. (1988). *Foucault* (S. Hand, Trans.). Minneapolis, MN: University of Minnesota Press.

Deleuze, G. (1990). *The logic of sense* (M. Lester, Trans.). New York, NY: Columbia University Press.

Deleuze, G. (1993). *The fold: Leibniz and the Baroque* (T. Conley, Trans.). Minneapolis, MN: University of Minnesota Press.

Deleuze, G., & Guattari, F. (1977). *Anti-Oedipus: Capitalism and schizophrenia*. (R. Hurley, M. Seem, & H. R. Lane, Trans.). New York, NY: Penguin.

Deleuze, G., & Guattari, F. (1987). *A thousand plateaus: Capitalism and schizophrenia* (B. Massumi, Trans.). Minneapolis, MN: University of Minnesota Press.

Denzin, N. K. (2005). The first international congress of qualitative inquiry. *Qualitative Social Work, 4*(1), 105–111. doi:10.1177/1473325005050205

Drewery, W. (2005). Why we should watch what we say: Position calls, everyday speech and the production of relational subjectivity. *Theory & Psychology, 15*(3), 305–324. doi: 10.1177/0959354305053217

Drewery, W., & Kecskemeti, M. (2010). Restorative practice and behaviour management in schools: Discipline meets care. *Waikato Journal of Education, 15*(3), 101–113. doi: 10.15663/wje.v15i3.85

Ecclestone, K. (2007). Resisting images of the 'diminished self": The implications of emotional well-being and emotional engagement in education policy. *Journal of Education Policy, 22*(4), 455–470. doi: 10.1080/02680930701390610

Ecclestone, K., & Hayes, D. (2009). Changing the subject: The educational implications of developing emotional well-being. *Oxford Review of Education, 35*(3), 371–389. doi: 10.1080/03054980902934662

Epston, D., & White, M. (1992). *Experience, contradiction, narrative and imagination: Selected papers of David Epston and Michael White 1989-1991.* Adelaide, SA: Dulwich Centre Publications.

Fish, V. (1999). Clementis's hat: Foucault and the politics of psychotherapy. In I. Parker (Ed.), *Deconstructing psychotherapy* (pp. 54–70). London, UK: Sage.

Foucault, M. (1972). *The archeology of knowledge.* London, UK: Tavistock Publications.

Foucault, M. (1980). *Power/knowledge: Selected interview and other writings.* New York, NY: Pantheon Books.

Foucault, M. (1981). So is it important to think? In J. D. Faubion (Ed.), R. Hurley (Trans.), *Power: Essential works of Foucault 1954-1984* (pp. 454–458). New York, NY: The New Press.

Foucault, M. (1982). Afterword: The subject and power. In H. Dreyfus & P. Rabinow (Eds.), *Michel Foucault: Beyond structuralism and hermeneutics* (pp. 199–226). Brighton, UK: Harvester Press.

Foucault, M. (1995). *Discipline & punish: The birth of the prison.* New York, NY: Random House.

Foucault, M. (1997). Polemics, politics, and problematizations (L. Davis, Trans.) In P. Rabinow (Ed.), *Ethics, Subjectivity, and truth, essential works of Foucault, 1954–1984* (pp. 111-121). New York, NY: The New Press.

Foucault, M. (2000a). Technologies of the self. In P. Rabinow (Ed.), *Ethics: Subjectivity and truth* (pp. 223–252). London, UK: Penguin.

Foucault, M. (2000b). The ethics of the concern for self as a practice of freedom. In P. Rabinow (Ed.), *Ethics: Subjectivity and truth* (pp. 282–302). London, UK: Penguin.

Foucault, M. (2000c). The subject and power. In J. D. Faubion (Ed.), *Power: Essential works of Foucault 1954-1984* (pp. 326–348). New York, NY: The New Press.

Freire, P. (1970). *Pedagogy of the oppressed.* London, UK: Penguin.

Frey, A., & Davis Doyle, H. (2001). Classroom meetings: A program model.

Children & Schools, 23(4), 212–222. doi:10.1093/cs/23.4.212

Furedi, F. (2009). *Wasted: Why education isn't educating.* London, UK: Continuum International Publishing Group.

Galloway, D., & Roland, E. (2004). Is the direct approach to bullying always the best? In P. K. Smith, D. Pepler, & K. Rigby (Eds.), *Bullying in schools: How successful can interventions be?* (pp. 37–53). Cambridge, UK: Cambridge University Press.

Gardner, H. (2006). *Multiple intelligences: New horizons.* New York, NY: Basic Books.

Geertz, C. (1983). *Local knowledge.* New York, NY: Basic Books.

Giroux, H. A. (2004). Critical pedagogy and the postmodern/modern divide: Towards a pedagogy of democratisation. *Teacher Education Quarterly, 31*(1), 31–47.

Gray, S. (2012). *Are they really at risk?: Students' stories of success.* Unpublished master's thesis, University of Waikato.

Gray, S., & Drewery, W. (2011). Restorative practices meet key competencies: Class meetings as pedagogy. *International Journal on School Disaffection, 8*(1), 13–21.

Hamilton, C., & Kecskemeti, M. (2015). Beginning teachers reflect on inclusive practices: "I didn't realize that he only had half a hand". *International Journal of Inclusive Education, 19*(12), 1265–1279. doi: 10.1080/13603116.2015.1055341

Harrison, R., Clarke, J., Edwards, R., & Reeve, F. (2003). Power and resistance in further education: The discursive work of negotiating identities. In J. Satterthwaite, E. Atkinson, & K. Gale (Eds.), *Discourse, power, resistance: Challenging the rhetoric of contemporary education* (pp. 57–70). Stoke on Trent, UK: Trentham Books.

Hill, J., & Hawk, K. (2005). *Achieving is cool: What we learned from the AIMHI project to help schools more effectively meet the needs of their students.* Albany, Auckland: IPDER Massey University.

Hook, D. (2003). Analogues of power: Reading psychotherapy through the sovereignty-discipline-government complex. *Theory and Psychology, 13*(5), 605–628. doi: 10.1177/09593543030135006

hooks, b. (1994). *Teaching to transgress: Education as the practice of freedom.* New York, NY: Routledge.

Hopkins, B. (2004). *Just schools: A whole school approach to restorative justice.* London, UK: Jessica Kingsley Publishers.

Hopkins, B. (2011). *The restorative classroom: Using restorative approaches to foster effective learning.* Milton Keynes, UK: Speechmark Publishing.

Hursh, D. (2003). Discourse, power and resistance in New York: The rise of testing and accountability and the decline of teacher professionalism and local control. In J. Satterthwaite, E. Atkinson, & K. Gale (Eds.), *Discourse, power, resistance: Challenging the rhetoric of contemporary education* (pp. 43–56). Stoke on Trent, UK: Trentham Books.

Kaveney, K., & Drewery, W. (2011). Classroom meetings as a restorative practice: A study of teachers' responses to an extended professional development innovation. *International Journal on School Disaffection, 8*(1), 5–12.

Kecskemeti, M. (2011). *A discursive approach to relationship practices in classrooms: An exploratory study.* Unpublished doctoral thesis, University of Waikato.

Kecskemeti, M. (2013). The stance of curiosity in the classroom: Is there a place for counselling skills in teachers' work? *New Zealand Journal of Counselling, 33*(1), 36–53.

Kecskemeti, M., & Hamilton, C. (2015). Uncovering precariosity using a circle conversation with counselling practitioners: The institutions are training the people but where is the work for them? *New Zealand Journal of Counselling, 35*(2).

Kecskemeti, M., Kaveney, K., Gray, S., & Drewery, W. (2013). A deconstructive approach to class meetings: Managing conflict and building learning communities. *Narrative and Conflict: Explorations in Theory and Practice, 1*(1), 30–52. doi: 10.13021/G8PP47

Lagermann, C. L. (2014). Sticky categorizations: Processes of marginalization and (im)possible mo(ve)ments of transcending marginalization. *International Journal of Qualitative Studies in Education, 27*(5). doi: 10.1080/09518398.2014.916012

Larner, G. (1999). Derrida and the deconstruction of power as context and topic in therapy. In I. Parker (Ed.), *Deconstructing psychotherapy* (pp. 39–53). London, UK: Sage.

Laws, C., & Davies, B. (2000). Poststructuralist theory in practice: Working with 'behaviourally disturbed' children. *International Journal of Qualitative Studies in Education, 13*(3), 205–222.

Leach, T., & Lewis, E. (2013). Children's experiences during circle-time: A call for research-informed debate. *Pastoral Care in Education: An International Journal of Personal, Social and Emotional Development, 31*(1), 43–52. doi: 10.1080/02643944.2012.702781

Macfarlane, A. H. (2004). *Kia hiwa ra!: Listen to culture: Māori students' plea to educators*. Wellington: New Zealand Council for Educational Research.

Marshall, M. (2001). Discipline without stress, punishment or rewards. *The Clearing House: A Journal of Educational Strategies, Issues and Ideas, 79*(1), 51-54.

Mazzei, L. (2004). Silent listenings: Deconstructive practices in discourse-based research. *Educational Researcher, 33*(2), 26–34. doi: 10.3102/0013189X033002026

Mazzei, L. (2014). Beyond an easy sense: A diffractive analysis. *Qualitative Inquiry, 20*(6), 742–746. doi: 10.1177/1077800414530257

McLaren, P., Martin, G., Farahmandpur, R., & Jaramillo, N. (2004). Teaching in and against the empire: Critical pedagogy as revolutionary praxis. *Teacher Education Quarterly, 31*, 131–153.

Ministry of Education. (2007). *The New Zealand curriculum: For English medium teaching and learning in years 1–13*. Wellington: Learning Media.

Ministry of Education. (2010). *Stand-downs, suspensions, exclusions and expulsions from school*. Wellington, New Zealand: Ministry of Education

Morgan, A. (2000). *What is narrative therapy?: An easy-to-read introduction*. Adelaide, SA: Dulwich Centre Publications.

Nelson, H. L. (2001). *Damaged identities; narrative repair*. London, UK: Cornell University Press.

Nickolite, A., & Doll, B. (2008). Resilience applied in school: Strengthening classroom environments for learning. *Canadian Journal of School Psychology, 23*(1), 94-113. doi: 10.1177/0829573508316596

Noguera, P. A. (2003). Schools, prisons, and social implications of punishment: Rethinking disciplinary practices. *Theory into Practice, 42*(4), 341–350. doi: 10.1207/s15430421tip4204_12

Parker, I. (1999). *Deconstructing psychotherapy*. London, UK: Sage.

Parker, I., & Shotter, J. (Eds.). (1990). *Deconstructing social psychology*. London, UK: Routledge.

Rabinow, P. (2000). Introduction: The history of systems of thought. In P. Rabinow (Ed.), *Ethics: Subjectivity and truth* (pp. xi–xlii). London, UK: Penguin.

Ransom, J. S. (1997). *Foucault's discipline*. Durham and London, UK: Duke University Press.

Restorative Practices Development Team, The. (2004). *Restorative practices for *schools*. Hamilton: University of Waikato.

Rogers, B. (2002). *Classroom behaviour*. London, UK: Paul Chapman.

Rogers, B. (2011). *Classroom behaviour: A practical guide to effective teaching, behaviour management and colleague support*. London, UK: Sage Publications.

Saltmarsh, S., & Youdell, D. (2004). 'Special sport' for misfits and losers: Educational triage and the constitution of schooled subjectivities. *International Journal of Inclusive Education, 8*(4), 353–371. doi: 10.1080/1360311042000259148

Santoro Gomez, D. (2008). Women's proper place and student- centred pedagogy. *Studies in the Philosophy of Education, 27*, 313–333. doi: 10.1007/s11217-007-9048-0

Satterthwaite, J., Atkinson, E., & Gale, K. (Eds.). (2003). *Discourse, power, resistance: Challenging the rhetoric of contemporary education*. Stoke on Trent, UK: Trentham Books.

Senge, P., Cambron-McCabe, N., Lucas, T., Smith, B., Dutton, J., & Kleiner, A. (2000). *Schools that learn*. London, UK: Nicholas Brealy Publishing.

Shacklock, G. (1998). Professionalism and intensification in teaching: A case study of 'care' in teachers' work. *Asia-Pacific Journal of Teacher Education, 26*(3), 177–189. doi: 10.1080/1359866980260302

Shildrick, M. (2000). Becoming vulnerable: Contagious encounters and the ethics of risk. *Journal of Medical Humanities, 21*(4), 215–227. doi: 10.1023/A:1009025125203

Shildrick, M. (2007). *Leaky bodies and boundaries: Feminism, postmodernism and (bio)ethics*. London, UK: Routledge.

Skiba, R. J., & Peterson, R. (1999). The dark side of zero tolerance: Can punishment lead to safe schools? *Phi Delta Kappan, 80*(5), 372–378.

Skiba, R. J., Michael, R. S., Carroll Nardo, A., & Peterson, R. L. (2002). The color of discipline: Sources of racial and gender disproportionality in school punishment. *The Urban Review, 34*(4), 317–342. doi: 10.1023/A:1021320817372

Slater, J. J., Fain, S. M., & Rossatto, C. A. (Eds.). (2002). *The Freirean legacy: Educating for social justice*. New York, NY: Peter Lang Publishing Inc.

Smyth, J., & Hattam, R. (2004). *Dropping out, drifting off, being excluded: Becoming somebody without school*. New York, NY: Peter Lang.

St Pierre, E. A. (2002). 'Science' rejects postmodernism. *Educational Researcher,*

31(8), 25–27.

St Pierre, E. A. (2004). Refusing alternatives: A science of contestation. *Qualitative Inquiry, 10*(1), 130–139. doi: 10.1177/1077800403259494

Sullivan, A. L. (2011). Disproportionality in special education identification and placement of English language learners. *Exceptional Children, 77*(3), 317–334. doi: 10.1177/001440291107700304

Teague, L. (2015). 'Acceptance of the limits of knowability in oneself and others': Performative politics and relational ethics in the primary classroom. *Discourse: Studies in the Cultural Politics of Education, 36*(3), 398–408. doi: 10.1080/01596306.2014.880047

Thorsborne, M., & Vinegrad, D. (2007). *Restorative practices and bullying: Rethinking behaviour management.* Queenscliff, VIC: Inyahead Press.

Timperley, H., Wilson, A., Barrar, H., & Fung, I. (2007). *Teacher professional learning and development: Best evidence synthesis iteration [BES].* Wellington: Ministry of Education.

Turrini, M., & Chicchi, F. (2013). Precarious subjectivities are not for sale: The loss of the measurability of labour for performing arts workers. *Global Discourse: An Interdisciplinary Journal of Current Affairs and Contemporary Thought, 3*(3–4), 507–521. doi: 10.1080/23269995.2014.885167

Watkins, M. (2007). Disparate bodies: The role of the teacher in contemporary pedagogic practice. *British Journal of Sociology of Education, 28*(6), 767–781. doi: 10.1080/01425690701610100

White, M. (1988). The externalising of the problem and the re-authoring of lives and relationships. *Dulwich Centre Newsletter, Summer.* Reprinted in M. White, & D. Epston (1990), *Narrative means to therapeutic ends,* New York, NY: W. W. Norton.

White, M. (1992). Deconstruction and therapy. In D. Epston & M. White (Eds.), *Experience, contradiction, narrative & imagination* (pp. 109–153). Adelaide, SA: Dulwich Centre Publications.

White, M. (1999). Reflecting teamwork as definitional ceremony revisited. *Gecko, 2,* 55–82.

White, M. (2007). *Maps of narrative practice.* New York, NY: W. W. Norton.

White, M., & Epston, D. (1990). *Narrative means to therapeutic ends.* New York, NY: W. W. Norton.

Winslade, J. (2005). Utilising discursive positioning in counselling. *British Journal of Guidance and Counselling, 33*(3), 351–364. doi: 10.1080/03069880500179541

Winslade, J. (2009). Tracing lines of flight: Implications of the work of Gilles Deleuze for narrative practice. *Family Process*, *48*(3), 332–346. doi: 10.1111/j.1545-5300.2009.01286.x

Winslade, J. (2013). From being nonjudgmental to deconstructing normalising judgment. *British Journal of Guidance and Counselling*, *41*(5), 518–529. doi: 10.1080/03069885.2013.771772

Winslade, J., & Monk, G. (2007). *Narrative counselling in schools: Powerful & brief* (2nd ed.). Thousand Oaks, CA: Corwin Press.

Winslade, J., & Williams, M. (2012). *Safe and peaceful schools: Addressing conflict and eliminating violence.* Thousand Oaks, CA: Corwin Press.

Index

A

activity, mixer   122, 124
ADHD   3, 64, 83
affect   115, 116, 155
Anderson and Goolishian (1992)   43, 54–6, 59
Andrew (case study)   43–8, 50–1, 54, 56–7, 58, 60, 150
anger as product of intra-action   81
anger management   66–7, 77–9
    case study   77–9
    programmes   64
Annamma, Boelé, Moore and Klingner (2013)   33, 34
Arribas-Ayllon, M and Walkerdine, V   100, 103
assumptions   99
autonomy and self-care   148
average, idealising of   33

B

Ball, S J   147
Barad, K   69, 115
    diffraction   154
Bateson, Gregory   50
behaviour, disruptive   1–2, 64, 120
behaviour management
    limitations of individual focus   23–4
    long-term v short term strategies   92–3, 104
    medical model   68–9
    positive behaviour approach   3–4
    restorative approach   66–7
    teacher-centred approach to   112
behaviour modification strategies   111

case study   5–6
    2–3
binary opposition   95, 103, 106, 121, 131–2, **132–3**
binary thinking   71
body language   125
bullying   43, 110–1
    anti-bullying programmes   112
    approaches to   48–9, 117
    victims of   28, 78
Burr, V   51–2, 53, 97
Butler, Judith   7, 26, 31–2, 33, 116–7

C

care, ethic of   140–1
care of the self   147–8, 155, **157**
case studies
    change as ongoing work (Amir and Glenn)   75–6
    discourses (Dillon)   150–2
    identity recognition *see also* Hannah   137–40
    knowledge and truth *see also* Andrew   43–8
    normalisation *see also* Matt   1–7
    positioning *see also* Robert   37–8
    positioning (Shane)   37–8
    re-authoring identity *see also* Tim   64–7
    sexual harassment *see also* Harry   17–24
    'special sport' class   28–30
    student-centred pedagogy *see also* Jacob and Leanne   90–2
categorisation *see also* naming   35
certainty as knowledge approach   43
change as ongoing work   74–6
children and thinking   117
circle conversations   113–8
citational practices   **40**

main points   39–40
citations, repetitive   16–7, 26, 37
   case studies   27–30, 75–6
   and dominant discourses   100
   positive   80
   responsibility for   35–6
citizenship education and relationship competencies   112
class meetings   56, 123–9
   case studies   4–5, 7, 9, 78–9
   as critique process   117–8
   organisation of   123–4
   research findings   129–30
classroom comunities   122
collegial conversations   163
colonisation, discourses of   25–6, 27, 143–4
compliance/ non-compliance *see* normalisation
conditions of possibility   106
confidentiality, code of   6
connection activities   122
counselling approach   4–5
critique   116–8, 120, 131, 144, 147, 156
curiosity   168
   as knowledge approach   43, 56–7, 58, 59

D

Davies, B
   conditions of possibility   95
   diffraction   154
   discourse, power of   99
   intra-action   81, 115–6
   normalisation   25, 33
   open listening   58
   repetitive citations   25, 26–7, 35–6, 37
   thinking skills   117
Davies, B and Gannon, S   115–6
Davies et al (2013)   31
deconstruction   164–6
   circle conversations as   121–3
   in class meetings   118–23
deconstruction approach
   main points   130–1
deferred consequences   3
Deleuze, G   72
Deleuze, G and Guattari, F   36, 58
   medical model of behaviour management   68–9
difference from norms   34, 115
diffraction   **157**
diffractive thinking   135–7, 154–6
Dillon (case study)   151–2
directed choice   3
disability and social judgement   28, 32
discourse knowledge   165
discourses   89–90, 97, 98
   colonising   143–4
   dominant   100
   dominant, critiquing of   165
   identification of   164
   of learning   97–8, 98–100, 102, 117, 132, **132–3**
      deconstruction and   120–1
   main points   156–7
   modes of engagement with   145–6
   and power relationships   151
   "seeping into consciousness"   99
diversity
   as deviation from norm   34
documents   80
Drewery, W   25–6, 27
drug abuse, parental   64–6

E

educational discourses *see* discourses of

learning
English lessons (case study) 90–2, 96, 101–3
ethics, professional 162, 164, 165
ethics, relational 152, 154
exclusion through documentation 80
exercises 15, 40–1, 62, 83–4, 107–8, 115, 130–3, 157–8
expertise as knowledge 47, 49, 54–5, 97, 102
  and exclusion 80
externalising 73–4, 82–3, **83**
  main points 82–3
  overview 63
externalising conversations
  case study 76–9
  four-part structure of 84–7

F
facilitator role in class meetings 124, 125
facilitators, onsite model 161, 162
focus groups 164, 166–7
Foucault, Michel 30
  discourse 98
  power 96, 100, 118
  power/knowledge 51–3
  problematisation 101
  reflection process 110
  "technologies of the self" 102, 146–9

G
gender relationships 44, 50
Gomez, Santoro 95–6
Gottwald, Klement 53

H
Hamilton, C and Kecskemeti, M 115
Hannah (case study) 137–40, 141–3, 144–5, 146–7, 151–5
Harry (case study) 17–24, 25, 26–7, 30, 31, 33, 36–7
Hopkins, B 122

I
identity 35
  alternative descriptions 67, 68, 74
  assigned 25, 26–7, 47, 67, 72–3
  constructed by discourse 99, 144–5
  mandated 71
  re-authoring of 63, 75–6, 77–9, 153, 155–6
  singular narratives 70–3
  teachers' professional 147, 148–9, 164, 167
inclusion and relationship competencies 112
information processing 55, 80
inquiry, two different approaches to **61**
interaction 9, 115–6
  rules of 119
internalising and externalising **83**
interpretation 49–50
  interpretive maps 50, 51
  as knowledge approach 48–9, 55–6, 57
intra-action 9, 69
  and anger 81
intra-active flow 115–6

J
Jacob and Leanne (case study) 90–2, 93, 95–6, 101–4, 105

K
karakia 124
Kecskemeti, M 118

Kecskemeti, M and Hamilton, C   117
key competencies, *The New Zealand
    Curriculum*   122
knowledge
    approaches to   42–3, 48–9, **61**
    different knowledges   52
    as expertise   102
    information processing   55, 59
    main points   60–1
    as power   51–4, 53, 97
    privileging of   49
    selective   50, 53–4
    students'   59–60
Kundera, Milan   53

L

labelling   72
labour: changing systems of   142
Lagermann, C L   71
    case study   75–6
language
    colonising   25–6
    externalising through   73
    as identity shaper   16–7, 67
    respectful   25–6
Leach, T and Lewis, E   32
Leanne *see* Jacob and Leanne
learning culture: disruption of   110–1
learning discourses *see* discourses of
    learning
learning environments   130
lines of flight   17
listening   57–8
    case study   137–40
    climate of   136
    quality of   151–3
    from stance of not knowing   150,
        166, 168

M

main points summaries
    citational practices   39–40
    deconstruction approach   130–1
    discourses   156–7
    externalising   82–3
    knowledge   60–1
    normalisation   13–4
    problematisation   106–7
mandated identity   71
Mandela, Nelson   99, 143–4
Māori cultural practices   113, 122
Māori students   34, 111–2
Matt (case study)   1–7, 8–9, 11
meaning-making as knowledge
    approach   56
meanings   25–6
    and consequences   23
    privileged   24
medical interventions (case study)   3
medical model of behaviour
    management   68–9
meeting formats and power
    relationships   113–4
mental health, teachers'   167
Midway High School (case study)
    160–2
Ministry of Education
    innovations grant   161
    learning concepts project   121–3
    restorative practice in schools   113
mixer activity   122, 124
moral order   26–7, 36, 99
moral values   32
Mystery Creek High (case study)   61,
    64–7, 76, 79
    intra-action support model   81

N

naming   23, 72
   and identity   25, 27–8, 67
   as "ongoing negative citation"
      16–7
   from power positions   24
Narelle and Jane (case study)   93–4
narrative frameworks   122, 166
narrative therapy model   126
narratives
   dominant   26–7
   incoherent   151–3
Nelson, H L   71
Nickolite, A and Doll, B   122
normalisation   7–9
   as coercive intervention   68
   and dominant discourse   144–5
   ideology of   33–4
   main points   13–4
   and minority groups   34
   and physical characteristics   32
   in school system   29–30
   through documentation   80
normalising judgements   13–4, **14**
   teachers and   169
normative requirements and social
      difference   115
North America and circles   113

O

observation as knowledge   48
ongoing repetitive citations *see*
      citations
open listening   57–8, 59–60, 61, 157
'others' as undesirables   28–9, 31–2, 60

P

'pants-pulling' case study   17–23
parent, effect of school intervention
      on   20–1
parenting, inadequate (case study)
      64–6, 69
Pasifika students   34
   cultural practices   122
pastoral care   44, 56, 58
pastoral care *see also* care
pedagogic strategy and quality of
      learning   93–4
pedagogy *see also* discourses of learning
      95–6
peer interactions, support for   122
peer mentoring   67, 80
peer support, teachers'   153–4
photography and truth   53
physical characteristics and
      normalisation   32
play as site of learning   103
positioning   36–9, 68, 150
   of teacher as expert   47–8
   of teacher identity   155
positioning *see also* identity; naming
positive behaviour approach   3–4, 6
Positive Behaviour for Learning
      (PB4L)   113
power   96
   productive   118–9
power/knowledge   51–4, 98–100
power positions   23, 24, 50
   gender-based   44
power relationships   54, 100
   challenged by deconstruction   165
   and meeting formats   113–4
   within schools   5, 20, 151
problem-solving, collaborative   163
problematisation   89, 101
   case study   103–4
   main points   106–7
   and teachers' identity   147
problematising discourses of teaching

and learning 107
problematising dominant ideas 132–3
professional learning 160–2
    teacher feedback 167–70
professionalism, discourse of 140
psychological assessment as behaviour management approach 68–9
punitive approaches 2–3, 65

Q

qualitative research 48, 135
quantitative research 48

R

Ransom, J S 145
rationality 136
recognition
    as control mechanism 31–2, 141, 144
    ethical responsibilities in 33
    and familiar discourse 146, 151
    through naming 25
refector role in class meetings 127
reflection 154
    in relationship-centred approach 163
reflection represents status quo 137
reflector role in class meetings 124
reflexivity 154
Reggio Emilia preschools 58
"regimes of truth" 51–2
relational approach 9–13, 14, 154
    key assumptions 10
relationality 33
relationship-centred approach 159–63
relationship competencies 112, 122
relationship maps 51
relationship problems in classrooms 110, 130
relationships, re-positioning of 78–9, 123
relationships and school discourses 89–90
relationships of power 98–9
repetitive citations *see* citations
repetitive speech 27
Resource Teacher: Learning and Behaviour (RTLB) 64
respect, language of 25–6
responsibility 69
restorative approach to behaviour management 4–5, 7, 9, 66–7
restorative practice in NZ schools 113
Restorative Practices Development Team 118, 126
restorative practices project 129–30
restorative principles and relationship-centred approach 159
rewards and recognition 2, 30–1, 32
Ritalin 3, 64
Robert (case study) 37–8, 38–9, 150
rule reminder 3

S

Saltmarsh, Sue 27
Saltmarsh, Sue and Youdell, D 28, 93
school discourses 89–90, 98–100
school systems and diffractive thinking 155
segregation 5, 8, 28, 34
selective inclusion of knowledge 53–4
self-care *see* care of the self
self-care and autonomy 148
Severe Behaviour Service 64
sexual harassment (case study) 17–23, 36–7
Shacklock, G 140–1

Shildrick, M 32, 33
smooth/striated spaces 36, 58, 73, 100
social models, media-driven 81–2
social skill training 112
socioeconomic background and student achievement 112
speaking positions 26
'special sport' class (case study) 28–30
"stance of curiosity" 43, 136
"stance of not knowing" 54–6, 57, 136, 150, 154, 168
status, relative *see* power
status quo 136, 137
  and truth technologies 149
Stoics and care of self 148
story writing *see* writing
"striated places" *see* smooth/striated places
student achievement and teacher-student relationships 111–2
student-centred pedagogy 95–6, 102–4
  changing status of 100
student resistance (case study) 90–2
student–student relationships 60, 81–2, 117
students in minority groups 34
students' relationship competencies 112
students' role in class meetings 126–7
students with disability 28

T

Te Kotahitanga programme 34
teacher-centred approaches to behaviour management 112
teacher-centred pedagogy 95–6, 98, 100

teacher–parent relationships 119
teacher role in class meetings 129
teacher–student interactions 37–8, 119–20, 151–2
teacher–student relationships 50, 57, 60, 169
  case study 90–2
  and discourses of schooling 89–90, 117, 118, 164
  and knowledge approaches 55
  and student achievement 111–2
teachers
  anxiety of beginning 12
  collegial relationships 17, 19, 21–2, 90, 169
  exploitation of 141–2
  feedback on professional learning 167–70
  professional identity of 147, 148–9, 155, 167
  role of 12–3
  as significant resource 162–3
  unrealistic expectations of 141–2
teachers, wellbeing of 170
  mental health 167
teachers' role in class meetings 127
teaching and learning: problematising discourses of 107
teaching practice
  case study 102–5
  and conditions of possibility 95
  diffractive thinking about 156
  ethics of 162
  problematisation of 105–6
  reflection on 135–6
Teague, Laura 150–2
"technologies of the self" 102, 146–9
The New Zealand Curriculum: key competencies 122

thinking skills   117
Thomas (case study)   150–1
Tim (case study)   64–9, 70–1, 72–3, 74, 76–81
transformative thinking   115
truth, regimes of   51–2, **107**
truth technologies   46–7, 49, 89, 146–9, 157, **157**
   case study   53–4
truth value   23
Turrini, M and Chicci, F   142

U
uniformity, privileging of   34

V
value judgments   31
violence, relational impact of   69

W
Watkins, M   93–5
White, M   72
White, M and Epston, D   49–50, 52, 70, 73–4
Winslade, J and Williams, M   122
workshops in relationship-centred approach training   163
writing, teaching of   91, 102–3, 103, 104
   case study   93–4
   problematisation   104–5
writing as alternative identity strategy   67, 79–80
writing in class meetings   129
writing *see also* English lessons

Y
Youdell, Deborah   27

Z
zero tolerance approaches   2, 5